BREAKING THE COLOR BARRIER

A Vision for Church Growth through Racial Reconciliation

Kevin R. Murriel

REDD HOUSE PUBLISHERS
BOOKS THAT MAKE A DIFFERENCE

ISBN-10: 0692396942
ISBN-13: 978-0692396940

ACKNOWLEDGMENTS

Writing this book has been a wonderful experience, and I have several people to thank for making the process memorable. I want to first thank my Lord and Savior Jesus Christ for making this experience possible.

I must thank two churches that understood the time commitment associated with research and writing and whose prayers and support are greatly appreciated. First, to Antioch United Methodist Church in Fairburn, GA, where I pastored when I began my studies at Duke, and secondly, to Cascade United Methodist Church in Atlanta, GA, where I served during the completion of this book and my doctoral degree at Duke. I am grateful to both congregations.

I greatly appreciate all of the professors in the Doctor of Ministry program at Duke Divinity School for their excellent instruction, and particularly Dr. Craig Hill for his leadership as director of the program. As a part of the first cohort in the DMin program, I am very thankful for his tireless work in making this the best experience it could be.

Certainly, writing this book out of my dissertation experience proved to be a very smooth process because I was blessed to have an amazing thesis supervisor. I thank Dr.

Richard Lischer for his insightful instruction and guidance through this process. It was a blessing to have a professor who is not only intelligent and knowledgeable of the subject matter, but who also pushed me to become a better researcher and writer. For Dr. Lischer, I am eternally grateful.

I want to thank my family and friends for their unwavering support and prayers during this process. I thank my parents and grandparents for the selfless sacrifices they made for me to have an education and other opportunities in life. I am forever grateful to you.

To my mentors, Bishop Woodie W. White and Reverend Dennis Grant for your prayers, counsel, and support; and to Dr. William Turner Jr., my second thesis reader, for your helpful insight in the final phase of this process. I am always thankful for you.

I also want to thank Rev. Edwin King, to whom I owe a great deal of gratitude for the hours spent in communication around the research for this book. Thank you for your prophetic spirit and for taking the extraordinary steps to help people see the need for racial reconciliation and equality in the world.

Last but certainly not least, I want to thank my beautiful wife, Dr. Ashleigh Murriel, for believing in and supporting God's plan for my life. You mean the world to me and I love and thank you for being my anchor during this process.

CONTENTS

FOREWORD

More than fifty years ago, prominent educator Dr. Benjamin Mays, president of the prestigious Morehouse College in Atlanta, Georgia, observed that in America, 11:00 on Sunday morning was the most segregated hour of the week! While that is less true today, it is the case that people at worship are more racially and ethnically separated than they are in most of their other daily activities.

In *Breaking the Color Barrier, A Vision for Church Growth through Racial Reconciliation*, Kevin Murriel addresses the issue of a racially divided Christianity at worship in an increasingly racially diverse America and world. It is uncomfortable territory for most Christians.

Segregation and racial division has dominated American life in general, and the Church in particular, especially at the congregational level, and adaptation to it as the norm has produced both justification for and comfort with it.

Some years ago, Kevin took a class with me, The Methodist Church and Race, when he was a student at Candler School of Theology at Emory University. There he was introduced to a remarkable Methodist minister, Rev. Edwin

King, a Civil Rights activist and uncompromising champion of racial justice.

Kevin was fascinated that this white Mississippian, a child of the South, could be such a tireless advocate for the elimination of segregation and the creation of a racially inclusive society and church. Little did I know that Kevin's interest would one day result in a doctoral dissertation, and now this published work.

It was in examining the ministry and commitment of King to an inclusive society, and especially an inclusive Methodist Church, that Kevin would conclude that race should no longer be a barrier for church life and organization, but indeed should be a basis of its witness, growth, and future.

In this book, we are reminded of the dramatic demographic change that is taking place in America. Quoting recent data, Murriel shares that by 2050, the American population will be 47% White, 29% Latino, 13% Black, and 9% Asian. The nation is and will be a far more racially diverse one than it is today.

How is the Church preparing for such a future, asks Murriel? Indeed, he challenges the church to see its future growth in its ability to embrace such diversity rather than ignoring or seeking to defy it.

The ultimate claim of Murriel, however, is not a sociological one but a theological one.

He, like King, calls the Church to remember its purpose. He points the reader to The Great Commission, "Go therefore and make disciples of all nations, baptizing them in the name of the Father, and of the Son and of the Holy Spirit; and teaching them to obey everything that I have commanded you" (Matthew 28:19-20).

Murriel recognizes that to change a pattern of congregational development and church growth from a principle of homogeneity to heterogeneity will not be easy. He offers suggestions to help pastors and laity move to new a way of evangelizing and establishing the congregation as a beloved community, where all of God's people are welcomed and embraced in their diversity- the gift of a creative God. He offers the role of reconciliation in this process; how to move from where we are to where we want to be. He assures that it will be hard work.

I have always been drawn to the Pentecost account found in Acts 2. This is considered the beginning of the Church. Those gathered were as diverse of a group as could be gathered at that time; racially, ethnically, culturally, even nationally. They even spoke different languages.

Yet, when the Holy Spirit came upon them, they found common ground and common purpose in worship and in the

Lordship of Jesus Christ. They became transformed into disciples who transformed the world. Murriel believes it can happen again.

In Breaking the Color Barrier, Kevin Murriel points the Church to its purpose and goal by looking back, so that it can move forward!

Bishop Woodie W. White
Bishop in Residence
Candler School of Theology
Emory University

PREFACE

The dialogue about race in American Christianity has shifted in the past 10 years. A new emphasis is being placed on an approach to Christian community that is more heterogeneous in nature than homogeneous. This will ultimately translate into more racially diverse congregations in many mainline Christian churches in the coming years.

The reality of such an emphasis must also consider the immense problem the United States of America continues to have with issues over race. Christianity in America is also connected to systems and institutions that continue to struggle over equality for all people. Such structures and institutions are primarily, but not limited to, schools and government agencies.

The issue of race in America, however, is not limited to the Church (as I will refer to Christianity in America for the extent of this book); but as racism, prejudice, and inequality is perpetuated through systems and institutions in America, the effect directly impacts the Church.

In this book, I will define the *Church* as the

one, holy, apostolic, and universal body of Jesus Christ. Relating to the imminent shift in diversity, the primary focus will be on individual church communities that make up the Church universal.

The demographics of the United States have changed rapidly since the late 19th century. This change is expected to continue through 2050.[1] According to national data, in the year 2050, the population of the United States will increase from 300 million to 438 million. In addition, whites will no longer be the majority, reflecting a population decrease from 67% to 47%. As this decrease occurs, there will be a rise in diversity within the United States.

According to the Pew Research Center, 19% of people in the United States will be foreign born by the year 2050. The Latino population is expected to increase from 14 to 29 percent, while the Asian population will increase from five to nine percent. Blacks, now 13 percent, are expected to remain the same.

Because of the racial transition occurring in America, it is inevitable that the Church will be affected in some way. Historically, America has wrestled with issues over race and inequality, and in effect, these tensions have directly impacted the nature of the Church and its ability to function as a diverse body of people that are truly united.

This book will not accept the divisions within America's racial history as inevitable, but will present a vision that will foster a movement towards racial reconciliation in light of the coming shift in America's racial and ethnic populations.

This vision will center on a significant civil rights figure and pastor–Rev. Edwin King–whose spiritual and social convictions led him to become one of the leading voices of racial equality and reconciliation in the South during the Civil Rights Movement and beyond.

The core of *Breaking the Color Barrier* will address the question prompted by ethnic diversity in America and the nature of the gospel itself: "Why is racial reconciliation essential to American Christian life, and how did Ed King–a white civil rights leader and pastor–model a way toward that goal for all of us to follow?"

This book argues that the Church, void of racial reconciliation, will fail to accomplish the Great Commission given by Jesus in Matthew 28:19 to "Go into all the world and make disciples of all nations," which will subsequently lead to a greater decline in mainline Christianity because of its inability to make the inevitable shift from homogeneous church communities to heterogeneous ones.

The theological implications associated with race and the Church are many. Racial reconciliation, I will argue, is a theological issue that is approached in sociological and ecclesiological contexts. It has to answer the questions:

- Why does the Church need to accept diversity?
- Who are the perpetuators of inequality, by what are they motivated, and how can their actions and intentions be shifted?
- When will the Church know that reconciliation has taken place?

The following chapters will seek to answer these questions not with a sense of finality, but with examples that allow for interpretation and application. That which has proved counterproductive to authentic Christian community will hopefully be challenged in an attempt to provide a model of racial reconciliation for Christians in America.

In order to set the framework for the vision that the life of Rev. Edwin King provides for racial reconciliation in American Christianity, I will trace national concerns around race (primarily in the South) that have existed from 1946 to today.

Chapter One will trace these national concerns from a historical context of racial tension out of which Ed King's background, social and theological convictions, and calling emerged.

To assist in understanding the landscape of racial division during the aforementioned time period, this chapter will draw on documented examples of violent racial acts committed against blacks in the South and the growing conflict surrounding civil rights and equality for all people.

This section will be primarily sociological and historical in nature, and will provide insight into the theological divisions in local church communities because of the societal divide. I will highlight groups such as SSOC and SNCC who were instrumental in the development and implementation of local and national demonstrations that raised societal awareness to the unacceptable actions behind racism. Briefly near the end of chapter one, I will introduce Rev. Edwin King into the narrative of these national concerns around race.

Chapter Two will focus primarily on the background, social and theological convictions, and calling of Rev. Ed King. As a man whose life would prove to be driven by racial conflict and eventually reconciliation, I will seek in this chapter to frame *how* the national tensions around race awakened his conscience to act in support of racial equality.

This chapter will provide Rev. King's definition of racial reconciliation and what it means for the Church universal. The context of the chapter is between 1946-1965, primarily in Mississippi and Alabama. It is in these two states that Rev. King participated in most of his demonstrations and also planned with other students, professors, and church and community leaders.

Chapter two will also discuss the immense challenges that Ed King, a white civil rights participant, experienced and how theologically that translated into his greater calling as a pastor and activist whose primary objective was to integrate churches and public facilities.

The model for racial reconciliation in American Christianity based on Ed King's life will be the focus of chapters 3-6. This model is divided into strategies that Ed King implemented to keep the nation conscious of racial injustice and inequality. Chapter three will explain the reasoning behind the level of intentional planning that had to be done before any demonstrations, etc. could occur.

It is here that I will provide an interpretation of the motivation behind this planning and the struggles that were overcome in pursuit of equality. Such planning would evolve to include populations of individuals who had great influence in society.

Students who attended colleges and universities, both black and white, would prove extremely instrumental to the model for racial reconciliation and in that time, racial equality. Without student involvement, the Civil Rights Movement may not have received the traction that it did.

Chapter 4 will focus on Ed King as a student at Millsaps College in Jackson, MS, and as a chaplain at Tougaloo College in Jackson, MS. It will also include his strategy for harnessing the energy and passion of college students into a concerted effort to bring about change.

The students who participated in organizations and demonstrations would be trained and joined by civil rights leaders, clergy and laity.

Chapter 5 will focus on the intended purpose of civil rights leaders, clergy, and laity in the struggle for racial equality. Included will be specific demonstrations that laid the foundation for an awakening of the conscience of citizens in Mississippi and Alabama to racial prejudice, and the need for reconciliation and change.

Most important to the demonstrations and the intentional planning were the outcomes they produced. Chapter 6 will focus on the change that occurred because of the model Ed King's life produced for racial reconciliation. The highlighted events will focus on the integration of churches, public facilities, and the subsequent impact they would have on society.

This chapter will also put into perspective the evolution of Ed King's calling as a pastor and how the challenges he faced eventually brought reconciliation to the Mississippi Methodist Conference that initially rejected him because of his stance on racial equality.

Chapter 7 will focus on Rev. King's eschatological perspective of the Church with particular emphasis on American Christianity. The key question that will be assessed is, "How does racial reconciliation or the lack thereof affect our perspective of the Kingdom of God and the life to come?"

The explanation of *why* Ed King pursued racial justice as his vocation is rooted in his understanding of eschatology and the imminent coming of the Kingdom of God on Earth and in heaven. As an indicator of the progress made through the model Rev. King's life provides, I will argue how the shift from homogeneous to heterogeneous American Christian communities affects racial reconciliation.

The final chapter will focus on *why*

pursuing racial reconciliation using Rev. Edwin King's life as a model will positively inform the Church's ability to make disciples for Jesus Christ in a multicultural society. The emphasis will be on what pastors, local churches, students, civic leaders, and citizens can do to participate in racial reconciliation to create a more inclusive culture to fulfill the mission of the Church universal.

The ending analysis will provide a vision for American Christianity that broadens the conversation of what Christians must do in a changing society to keep the Church a thriving movement in the world.

Breaking the Color Barrier

CHAPTER 1

Racial Tension in America's South

The obstacles to racial harmony in America can be traced to historic struggles in U.S. School systems. In 1954, the U.S. Supreme Court handed down the famous Brown v. Board of Education decision outlawing state-mandated separate schools for black and white students. Since that decision, hundreds of American school districts, if not more, have attempted to implement desegregation plans.

In the early years of desegregation, most of these plans focused on the South and resulted in the most integrated schools being located in the South by the early 1970s.[2] The period between 1954 and 1970, however, showed little improvement in race relations, particularly in the South.

In the wake of the Brown v. Board of Education and the 1955 Montgomery bus boycott, a civil rights movement seemed ready to take off. But during the nearly three years following the bus boycott's conclusion in 1956, civil rights activism had stalled.

The student-led sit-ins revived the movement, harnessing mass protest as an effective weapon, providing every black American with a sense of involvement. This revival reached into the farthest corners of the South, and began tugging at the conscience of the nation.[3]

One such group of students that organizationally led the charge for equality in the South was The Southern Student Organizing Committee (SSOC). In Mississippi, the students in SSOC concentrated most of their efforts on repairing and rebuilding the damaged and destroyed community centers decimated by white supremacy groups. Their efforts spread throughout cities around the South and had a critical impact.

The impact of their demonstrations, as will be discussed more thoroughly in the coming chapters, was not only felt in the South, but also in places where racial prejudice, for many, was an afterthought. Significant to this history were the Woolworth sit-ins in Greensboro, North Carolina, in 1961 (also noted in coming chapters), which provide an extraordinary model of non-violent protest.

The heroic actions taken by many students, however, did not come without cost. In 1968, students at South Carolina State College, along with others, attempted to desegregate the All Star Bowling Lanes in Orangeburg. The students' efforts were met with resistance, eventually leading to three tense evenings in the city.

On the fourth night, February 8th, students and community members demonstrated near campus while officers patrolled the area. South Carolina highway patrolmen eventually opened fire on the demonstrators, killing two SCSC (South Carolina State College) students and one high school student. Twenty-seven others were wounded.[4]

A memo from SSOC written in April 1964 states: "We as young Southerners, hereby pledge to take our stand now to work for a new order, a New South, a place which embodies our ideals for all the world to emulate, not ridicule. We find our destiny as individuals in the South in our hopes and our work together as brothers."[5]

Resolve to stay in the fight for freedom,

though not easy, was the best option blacks in America had. To quit was to give up their humanity and neglect the importance of their trust in God.

The SSOC had to be very methodical in their approach. Such an approach committed SSOC to developing campus service and educational programs designed to awaken white southern students to problems on campus and in the community, and to draw these students into the movement for social change.

SSOC also advocated that the students take their activism off campus, suggesting that they join community organizing projects at the coalition level not only in the Negro community, but also in disinherited predominately white communities. The projects would revolve around the issues of unemployment, low wages, union organization, poverty, lack of community facilities, etc.[6] If the movement to build community was going to work, it would take a unified effort from whites and blacks.

SNCC (The Student Non-violent Coordinating Committee) also played an important role in the organization of students to bring awareness to racial inequality in America. Minutes of the meeting of the SNCC Executive Committee, December 27-31, 1963, show that a part of their mission was to be as organized and effective as possible before pursuing action. Ella Baker, in this meeting, suggested that SNCC placed too much value on action and not enough on planning.[7] She said,

> Perhaps our Coordinating Committee structure is obsolete. Do we need a small policy making group, a legal advisory board to plan long range strategy? How do we handle education, both within and beyond SNCC–new staff? Conferences? Perhaps we should begin making specific national demands such as a national economic planning commission.[8]

Issues on inequality all over the South emerged from these meetings and others. Bob Moses of Mississippi commented in 1963 that the government estimated a $50,000 capital investment was needed to realize $3-4,000 net in farming, and felt that the only hope for the small farmer was to salvage some of the small white farmers, abandoning the Negroes. And the people leaving the farms were not only unemployed, but also largely unemployable.

Mississippi during that time had a few experimental programs. In Ruleville, there was a self-help project making quilts where women earned up to 30 cents an hour. In Amite County there was the possibility of a syrup-making project that the government eventually opposed. Food and clothing programs were essential because if they could guarantee food and clothing, black people in areas of the South, where political action was needed, would not move North in search of support and could be organized into groups that could effect change.

Inasmuch as inequality proved to be the overarching issue among blacks and whites in America, violence and ill treatment of blacks in the South soon became the reality the nation would have to confront. SNCC organized itself such that students and staff became the catalyst for many of the demonstrations that in most cases turned into violent attacks on those demonstrating.

These demonstrations were aimed at registering blacks to vote, eating at white owned restaurants, and providing equal opportunity for blacks in the workforce. We should not, however, ignore the level of harm that was legally and physically inflicted on blacks (those in SNCC and other affiliates) during and after these demonstrations.

On August 15, 1961, in Amite County, Bob Moses, an SNCC registration worker, and three Negroes who had tried unsuccessfully to register to vote in Liberty, were driving toward McComb when a county officer stopped them. He asked if Moses was the man "who's been trying to register our niggers." All were taken to court and Moses was arrested for "impeding an officer in the discharge of his duties," fined $50, and he spent two days in jail.[9]

Police also participated in the brutality of black demonstrators. On July 5, 1962, in Jackson Hinds County, Jesse Harris, 20, and Luvaghn Brown, 17, SNCC workers, charged that they were beaten and threatened with death while serving a 30-day sentence in the county jail for contempt of court.

The young men had refused to move from a court bench customarily occupied by whites while they were attending the trial of Mrs. Diane Nash Bevel. The young men said that in the courthouse elevator, a deputy sheriff called Harris "a damned nigger" and beat him about the head with his fist.

At the county farm, they were singled out as freedom riders and wore striped uniforms. Both were beaten by guards; Harris was beaten with a length of a hose while other prisoners held him.[10]

The theologian Reinhold Niebuhr, writing in 1932, claimed that although there were many white people who identified with the "Negro" cause, the "white race" as a whole could not admit blacks to equal rights until they were forced to.[11]

Until whites were forced to treat blacks equally, even places of worship treated blacks as inferior and denied them access. Public opinion polls in the mid-1950s showed whites in Mississippi overwhelmingly opposed integration.

Rev. Ed King, who at the time was a young Methodist minister and civil rights activist, understood too well the period when racial extremism took hold in Mississippi. He says,

> No one thought real change [in race relations] would come any time soon. But [our] teachers, especially in the Methodist church, felt free to talk about it in the late '40s and '50s. By the middle 1950s, anybody in the white community who raised questions [about segregation] was accused of being a communist. Ministers who could have raised the questions with me in 1948 or '50–by 1955 or 1956 were losing their pulpits and being driven out of the state.[12]

Fueled by Jim Crow laws that mandated the separation of blacks and whites in public facilities, tension over the effects of such laws sparked outrage among blacks in the South. This was the crucible of Rev. Edwin King's ministry of racial equality and reconciliation.

As a child in Vicksburg, Mississippi, he had lived the same kind of segregated life as any other white Southerner. He learned the "racial facts of life" early.[13] His family values, however, were much different from those of many of his peers.

He was taught that he was superior not to people but to hate and resentment, and that no member of the King family should look on others with condescension. He was told to use good manners, courtesy, the Golden Rule, and to revere "traditional American beliefs about democracy, justice, and equality.[14]"

King grew up watching blacks, as hired hands, work under harsh conditions. Black men and women were to King, nameless faces that endured the patient oppression of servitude in hopes of survival. Blacks would walk from their homes in the hollows up to the elegant homes of whites on the hills to work and then back down to reside.

King recalls the dilapidated homes that blacks lived in, which in many instances caught on fire or collapsed because of their poor structural conditions. The deaths of many blacks who King knew occurred as a result of collapsed or torched homes.

Troubled by the late night sounds of fire engines and screams for help "at the bottom of the hill," King began to imagine a life were everyone was equal–socially, religiously, and economically–even in the racially divided state of Mississippi.

CHAPTER 2

Reverend Ed King

In Junior High School, Ed King's teachers asked the pivotal question regarding the fires in the black neighborhoods: "Why do you think there are more fires in their neighborhoods than in ours?"[15] Whites from Ed's neighborhood would take old clothing to blacks whose homes had been destroyed in an effort to show their compassion for the black community.

Ed King knew, however, that there was a deeper issue to confront.

As news stories of the conflict in Germany and the holocaust continued to circulate around the world, and as racial tension mounted in his community, Ed King thought about becoming a pacifist in order to promote peace in the midst of racial conflict.

Pacifism, especially among white pastors in Mississippi during Ed King's childhood, was very common. In most cases, especially when racism subdued any notion of reason or social change, white pastors got a pass on standing up for equality because they wanted to "keep the peace."

King would eventually discover that a calling to pacifism would not be consistent with the role he would be chosen by God to uphold in the movement for equality for blacks in Mississippi and in the greater Civil Rights Movement in America. The reality of the death camps of Jews during the holocaust and the extreme disregard for the humanity of blacks in Mississippi ignited Ed's passion to pursue his calling as an activist.

Ed King listened intently to his teacher at MYF (Methodist Youth Fellowship) as she spoke about how harshly America historically treated the Native American people and how that correlated to how whites in Mississippi treated blacks.

The problem, however, with white ministers speaking to these issues, is that it was almost guaranteed that they would lose their pulpits, and in many cases, be driven from the town. Yet Ed King continued to listen to the prophetic voice of his MYF teacher as she spoke words that convicted him and caused him to think about what he could do to be a part of the change that needed to take place.

Ed King was in his 12th grade Civics class at his high school in Vicksburg when the Brown v. Board of Education decision was handed down. He indicates, "the Methodist kids and the Episcopalian kids had been discussing the case and its implications for two years."[16]

Most people in the community and around the South were surprised by the decision; however, Ed King and the group of young people who had been discussing the case believed that something would change, and they were prepared to act if the case was in favor of desegregation.

The segregated white Methodist church in Mississippi prepared Ed King for a new perception of race and social order. This segregated religious experience broadened his social vision of a new order that would encompass equality for all.

The discovery that the national church held views radically different from those of his fellow white Mississippi Methodists raised unsettling questions in King's mind about the faith of his fathers and the theological presuppositions of the closed society.[17]

As early as 1944, the General Conference of the Methodist Church had stated that "no race is superior or self-sufficient" and had proudly affirmed the equal protection of all races "through the agencies of law and order."[18]

As King began to question the system of the Methodist church in Mississippi, issues with his family began to trouble him. He began to have doubts about his father and mother because of their reluctance to follow through on their admonitions of toleration and decency.

King believed there was something wrong with people–particularly his parents and those in his church–who preached love for all humanity but whom, at the same time, forced him, with direct and indirect threats of shunning and shame, to renounce love and to distance himself from blacks.[19]

There were very few clergy, as King recalls, that got together during this time to make statements against segregation or the treatment of blacks in Mississippi. King says, "I knew by the end of high school about fights and debates in the Methodist (General) Church and that pastors that spoke out about race issues were considered communists and they and their families were attacked."[20]

The mood among clergy, black and white, was that of hysteria and fear when it came to speaking against segregation in America. People focused mostly on the racial climate in the South, but racial inequality, from King's perspective, was a national issue. King's interest in history came from his experience as a child playing on the battlefields in Vicksburg, Mississippi. He believed that slavery was wrong and as he got older, understood that the American political system fostered much of the separation among races in America.

Knowing that the American political system could not find a democratic way to end slavery because of its capitalistic implications, King did not want the "new" change to come with the same military violence as that of the civil war. If desegregation and equality for all people became a reality, King was convinced that it would have to be done non-violently. His fear of change happening through violence was that the country would have to spend the next 100 years dealing with the aftermath.

Ed King did not seek the approval of his parents to pursue his vocation in civil rights, and in the fall of 1954, he entered Millsaps College. During this transition, King pondered the most pivotal questions of his life concerning his call to ministry, his collegiate career, and his involvement in civil rights.

Millsaps had a close relationship with Tougaloo College–a predominantly black college in Jackson, Mississippi. Audrey

Goodman, King's freshman English teacher at Millsaps, had once taught at Tougaloo. Goodman was from one of the dominant families in Jackson, and her brother was one of the city prosecutors. Goodman, also an active participant in the Methodist Women, was regarded as eccentric and understood well the problems with segregation.

During the year, white students would commute to Tougaloo for meetings to discuss what a desegregated society could look like and what role they could play in this change. Contact between black and white students was critical in the process of desegregation, particularly as the Civil Rights Movement intensified.

Ed King recalls that the students from Millsap's interaction with students at Tougaloo were safer than interactions with other black colleges around Mississippi, like Jackson State University and Alcorn State University. Because of the progressive nature of some in their student body, King notes that Medgar Evers talked to him about how important it was for him as an Alcorn State student to have contact with white students and faculty at Millsaps.[21]

By the spring of 1954, there was increasing pressure from other white colleges in Mississippi such as Ole Miss not to bring their students to the interracial meetings at

Millsaps. The more formal name of the interracial alliance that was being formed in colleges in Mississippi was the Intercollegiate Fellowship. The president of the Intercollegiate Fellowship was Tougaloo professor C.B. Lawyer, and Ed King himself served as secretary.

But the driving force of the interracial alliance was Tougaloo professor Ernst Borinski, a Jewish humanist who fled Nazi Germany in 1938. After service with the U.S. Forces in the war and later earning his doctorate in sociology, Borinski picked Tougaloo College as a fitting home for his radical scholarship and activism.[22]

In the basement of a class building, Borinski taught Ed King and other students theories about racial justice and social order. The bi-monthly meetings of the Intercollegiate Fellowship proved effective in igniting the passion of the students to pursue racial justice until the White Citizens' Council learned of the meetings.

Immediately, pressure was placed on administrators at the participating schools to disband the Intercollegiate Fellowship. Because of the pressure from the Citizens' Council, by the fall of 1957, the black students had dropped out of the Fellowship and by King's senior year, the Fellowship itself had disbanded.

Individual white teachers were threatened, and several lost their jobs because of their participation in the Fellowship. This, however, did not stop King and other students from continuing their pursuit of racial equality.

In a commencement address to Millsaps College students in 2005, King asserted:

> My graduation here at Millsaps was with the class of 1958. That year was, perhaps, the worst in Millsaps' history. We were under secret police surveillance and constant threat. The President of Millsaps, Dr. Ellis Finger, had personally defied the white racists of the Citizens' Council and refused to give them a religious endorsement of segregation, something done publicly by leaders at nearby white church liberal arts schools. By 1958 state censorship covered all public colleges; no speaker could be invited to campus even for a single class without approval of the state government. After massive media attacks and the specter of red baiting, even Millsaps had to publicly apologize for pro integration opinions and had to cancel scheduled speakers.[23]

King, seeing the people he thought should do something about segregation and racial injustice do nothing, felt convicted to do something himself. He was inspired by the words they called the "Millsaps National Anthem," the anti-slavery and anti-authoritarian government hymn of James Lowell (also the favorite hymn of Dr. Martin Luther King Jr.):

> Once to every man and nation, comes the moment to decide, In the strife of truth with falsehood, for the good or evil side; Some great cause, some great decision, offering each the bloom or blight, And the choice goes by forever, 'twixt that darkness and that light.
>
> Then to side with truth is noble, when we share her wretched crust, Ere her cause bring fame and profit, and 'tis prosperous to be just; Then it is the brave man chooses while the coward stands aside, Till the multitude make virtue of the faith they had denied.
>
> By the light of burning martyrs, Christ, Thy bleeding feet we track, Toiling up new Calv'ries ever with the cross that turns not back; New occasions teach new duties, time makes ancient good uncouth, They must upward still and onward, who would keep abreast of truth.
>
> Though the cause of evil prosper,

yet the truth alone is strong; though her portion be the scaffold, and upon the throne be wrong; yet that scaffold sways the future, and behind the dim unknown, standeth God within the shadow, keeping watch above His own.[24]

King refused to be a pacifist, but he also knew that participating in the movement could cost him his life and reputation among whites in the South–a chance he was willing to take. His core conviction, however, was that "no matter what happened the hand of the Lord was in it."[25]

A close friend of Ed King, Medgar Evers, who would eventually lead the civil rights struggle in Jackson, came to the area in the Fall of 1954. Evers had just become head of the NAACP, and he and King met on the campus of Tougaloo College at one of the interracial meetings.

In the summer of 1954, the response of the white south shifted as the Southern Baptist Convention made a statement to support the Brown v. Board of Education decision. The SBC acclaimed the Supreme Court's decision as being "in harmony with the constitutional guarantee of equal freedom to all citizens, and with the Christian principles of equal justice and love for all men."[26]

This decision gave King hope that a large, prominent group could take a stance on a nationally pressing issue like segregation and affect some sort of change–the theory King believed would work better than just individual witness. However, not much came from the SBC's statement and many things remained the same.

Soon thereafter, in July of 1955, a black minister was murdered in a white neighborhood in Mississippi and King recalls that the white police did nothing to seek justice in the crime. King became aware that he had the option of pursuing his vocation in civil rights through a civic or an ecclesial avenue.

He chose to go the ecclesial route as a minister because in the Deep South, most people involved in government, etc. were affiliated with the church. He did not see then much separation.

The church people were the school board and other public officials and King believed that they would take seriously their Christian values and live them out through their civic responsibilities; but this was not the reality.

King thought simplistically. He presumed that if white clergy, like some did, could refuse to give the invocation at Citizens' Council meetings, they would at least get a group together and make a public statement against segregation. But out of fear for their families and their jobs, this did not happen.

The lack of action from those who claimed to be Christians, and their unwillingness to uphold the values of Christ, were enough to propel King into a committed vocation as a minister of the Gospel with a specific calling to civil rights.

His awareness of ministers that had suffered as martyrs for speaking out against racial injustice helped to guide his vision for what a strategy for change and reconciliation could look like. He believed that the best approach to change would be a concerted effort of a group rather than just individual action.

King graduated in May of 1958 from Millsaps College with a degree in English literature. By the time he had graduated, he was certain of his future in pursuing racial justice. Being prepared theologically to deal with the implications of this chosen life, he enrolled in Boston University's School of Theology.

Dr. Martin Luther King Jr., who also attended Boston University, gained the attention of Ed King with his leadership and involvement in the Civil Rights Movement. The non-violent philosophy of Dr. King and his ability to organize groups to pursue racial justice served as a catalyst for Ed King's decision, although it put him in conflict with his parents and the Mississippi Methodist Church.

At Boston, Ed King also studied with the black theologian and dean of Marsh Chapel, Howard Thurman, whose reflections on prayer and mysticism profoundly shaped his own deliberate piety.[27]

Through the consortium of theological schools called the Boston Theological Institute, King attended lectures by Paul Tillich and Reinhold Niebuhr, who both taught at Harvard at the time. Niebuhr introduced King to the theologies of Karl Barth and Dietrich Bonhoeffer.

The writings of these theologians helped King nurture a confessional radicalism that balanced theological integrity with political involvement.[28]

Because of the heightened conflict during the movement in the 1960's, King decided to take a sabbatical from Boston and volunteer in Montgomery, Alabama. He did this just after the first Woolworth store sit-ins and suddenly, the theoretical perspective of racial justice became Ed King's life reality.

At the core of King's convictions, he knew that although pursuing racial justice would be a hard fight and cause division, his ultimate vision for American Christianity was that all races be united and reconciled through Jesus

Christ.

King's experience of segregated churches in Mississippi was his primary agitator; he wanted all churches integrated and open to all people. Ed King's definition of racial reconciliation does not suggest that all congregations must be diverse, however, his objective was to make sure congregations, when presented with the opportunity, were open to racial inclusivity and equality.

For King, racial reconciliation is a threefold process that must include the spiritual and social conviction of those fostering racial injustice and exclusivity, intentional planning and integration of the church and society, and the eschatological perspective of what racial justice can promote in the Kingdom of God.

During the 1960's, as communism disturbed areas of the country, a large obstacle that King and other civil rights leaders had to face was the racists suggesting they were trying to protect Christianity from individuals who sought equality for all people–a thought many deemed communist ideology.

Therefore, Ed King was very selective of the groups he joined that fought for racial justice out of concern that he would be labeled a communist and thus hinder any positive progress. The thought of many that the Deep South was the front line of Christianity, and that Christianity's ability to thrive depended on the South not giving into the communists was also a battle King and others faced.

The popular ideology (and even theology) that people would be segregated in heaven would provide another hurdle King and other activists would have to overcome. Though King didn't believe it, this perspective added a spiritual dimension that helped racists warrant segregation.

As a result, King knew something deeper needed to occur–something that would convict the core of a persons humanity and spirituality.

CHAPTER 3

Spiritual and Social Conviction

The transformations in Mississippians' lifestyles during the fifties did not introduce meaningful changes in the practice of racial segregation. In entertainment arenas, blacks and whites remained separated, for example in the maintenance of the upstairs "colored" galleries in the movie houses and the practice of setting certain times, if any, for African Americans to attend fairs and other festivals. Even at athletic events, the teams as well as the observers were either all black or all white.[29]

The issue, however, that attracted the most attention nationally during King's tenure at Millsaps was the brutal killing of Emmett Till, who had arrived from Chicago to visit family members in Leflore County, Mississippi. After hearing reports that Till was murdered because he jokingly whistled at a white woman in the town of Money "to prove" to his Mississippi cousins that he had white girlfriends back home in Chicago, the black community was enraged.

With the decision in September 1955 to acquit the two white men accused of kidnapping and murdering Till, the Civil Rights Movement was fueled and Ed King became one of its key leaders.

It was the opportune time to prepare and move forward with action as national coverage of the Emmett Till killing raised concerns throughout the nation about violence against African Americans by whites in Mississippi. Also exposed via newspaper and television were the disparities between Mississippi and other states in standards of living and illiteracy rates.[30]

The strategy for racial reconciliation that Ed King would eventually produce first included intentional planning that would arouse the spiritual and social convictions of white Americans. King's deepest questions and understanding of life came from his Millsaps teachers and friends.[31] Professors at their interracial gatherings taught him that nothing positive could be accomplished through renegade tactics and a lack of knowledge regarding the people and the racially induced system they would be standing against.

The planning would not be limited to a strategy to desegregate churches (although that was King's ultimate goal), but would also include ways to bring spiritual and social conviction to everyday citizens perpetuating a segregated society. In essence, for change to occur, the perpetuators of racial injustice would have to become participants in their own transformation.

The fall of 1960 was a challenging time nationally as many students found themselves caught between school and activism. Many were looking forward to graduation just a few months down the road.[32] The students were trained to participate in sit-ins and to protest non-violently, which made their commitment to discipline during the struggle just as viable as the education they sought to complete.

Racial Reconciliation as a Conscious Choice

Ed King and others made the conscious choice to participate in the Civil Rights Movement. King often spoke about fear and how it must be overcome in order for reconciliation to occur among any group of people. King's assertion about the ability to overcome fear and act in love leads ultimately to knowing joy.[33] He says,

> I am a veteran of the Civil Rights Movement and the anti-war Movement. We sang, "We Shall Overcome," but always with the next verse, "We are not afraid." But we really were afraid, sometimes terrified, and had to sing, with humility, not arrogance, "God is on our side." This anthem has been sung around the world from the Tahir Square in Cairo in the Arab Spring to Tiananmen Square in China, from the old Berlin Wall to the new Wall in Palestine. Many who are inspired by these verses don't recognize the scriptures so well known to the black church folk of Mississippi in 1960. In Psalm 56 David cries, "Be merciful to me, Oh God," and tells of his enemies and their power. "Whenever I am afraid I will trust in you. In God have I put my trust; I will not fear...When I cry out to you, then my enemies will turn back; this I know because God is for me." God is on our side.[34]

Ed King's strategy for racial reconciliation took into account the societal and spiritual implications of deep southern culture and what would need to happen in order for desegregation to occur. King, however, was placed in a somewhat awkward position.

He understood God's calling for him to be involved in Civil Rights would be non-conventional. A white southerner seeking ordination in a racially divided denomination (then the Methodist Episcopal Church South), while also working tirelessly to desegregate the same denomination was not only non-conventional, but most perceived it to be dangerous. God, however, would not allow Ed King to take this journey alone.

"Medgar Evers became a friend and guided me like an older brother[35]," King says. Evers encouraged King and also admired the work the he and the students at Millsaps accomplished through the interracial gatherings.

In a television speech given by Medgar Evers in Jackson in 1963, he said, "Let me appeal to the consciences of many silent, responsible citizens of the white community who know that victory for democracy in Jackson will be a victory for democracy everywhere."[36]

Evers' appeal to Mississippians underscored accurately what the movement would be about–persuading people by convicting their conscience toward human dignity in order to bring about social transformation. This was the message that Dr. Martin Luther King Jr. acclaimed, for example, in his speech at the Freedom Rally in Cobo Hall where he said:

> And this is why I've said that in order to get this bill (the Civil Rights Bill) through, we've got to arouse the conscience of the nation and we ought to march to Washington more than a hundred thousand in order to say that we are determined, and in order to engage in a nonviolent protest to keep this issue before the conscience of the nation. And if we will do this we will be able to bring that new day of freedom into being. If we will do this we will be able to make the American dream a reality.[37]

Dr. Martin Luther King Jr. was another person who accepted Ed King and became another guide and older brother to him.[38] Ed King took this "theology of the conscience" and applied it to the planning of events that would eventually take place in Jackson and around the south that led to the desegregation of white churches and began the process of racial reconciliation that continues even today.

Racial Reconciliation as Theological

If the consciences of white citizens were convicted, their hearts changed, and blacks and whites lived together in mutual respect, then for Ed King, the will of God for humanity was being fulfilled. Theologically, King believed the community of faith and the people of God as the Body of Christ lived out its beauty through its diversity.

He affirmed that we are all created in the Image of God and that the nature of the Church as the one, holy, apostolic, and universal church is to be lived unapologetically by showing love and extending grace toward all people. This was the ultimate goal of the struggle for racial equality.

In 1963, after black leader Aaron Henry ran for Governor and Ed King ran for Lt. Governor of Mississippi, former president of Alcorn College, P.S. Bowles, reached out to King.

King notes, "Like Medgar, this man saw my white soul as worth saving. He wanted me to understand history, as Faulkner said, 'The past is never forgotten; it's never even past.'"[39]

King's approach to racial reconciliation

was tied to the redemptive history that came through the death, burial, and resurrection of Jesus Christ that redeemed and continues to redeem the souls of humanity. God's redemptive power is still realized today as this, for King, is what leads to the spiritual and social convictions of people perpetuating racial injustice.

When Ed King was 19 years old, he tried to make sense of how men who were pillars of the church (primarily white Methodist churches) could treat blacks so inhumanly and participate in various killings of blacks in the south. He would continue to wrestle with this even as progress was made in the movement towards racial justice.

The theological mounds that King and other civil rights activists would have to overcome were many. King recalls a white man after the Emmett Till killing quoting Romans 8:28, "And we know that God causes all things to work together for good to those who love God, to those who are called according to His purpose," as if this was theological and scriptural justification for Till's murder.

The drive that kept King and other activists in pursuit of racial reconciliation was their Christian obligation to the Great Commission given by Jesus. Simply put, they were followers of Christ, and therefore the only justification they needed to pursue racial reconciliation was linked to the understanding that "this is what followers of Jesus Christ do."

Followers of Jesus Christ should live in harmony and community with all people regardless of their race. This is the reality of the ecclesia, and when it is promoted and practiced in society, we see a glimpse of the Kingdom of God here on Earth.

If the Church promoted the message of Jesus Christ accurately and effectively, then King believed that perpetuators of racial injustice would experience a life-changing spiritual conviction that would ultimately lead to a social transformation.

Motivation to Plan

It was time to do something radical. Overshadowed by the death of Emmett Till and other blacks in Mississippi, and perplexed by constant unfair treatment, Ed King and other students at the surrounding Jackson colleges moved forward. They could do nothing, however, without planning.

What they also came to understand was that taking on the entire racist establishment would be too great of a challenge. Therefore, King and the other students had to find a cause to rally around that would be impactful, yet manageable enough to put a dent in the racist establishment in their immediate context. This cause would be desegregating the white churches in Jackson, Mississippi.

If white churches could be desegregated, then the civic and educational leaders who attended those churches would be impacted and perhaps help lead the charge for change in other areas of society.

Notably, the church, as the center of religious and civic life in the 1960's in Mississippi, was a brilliant target for action, but was also very risky. For King, racial reconciliation occurs when a specific goal is set and around that goal, precise, intentional planning is conducted. King notes, "You have to find small ways to do things. If the crisis is great, you sometimes have to do different things."[40]

King and other students also wanted to make sure they followed the primary message of the leader of the Civil Rights Movement, Dr. Martin Luther King Jr., in how they pursued their plan of action. Medgar Evers also informed Ed King that he (King) had to find a way to stay in Mississippi and regardless of the tension, keep the strength to remain committed to their cause.

At Boston University, a dear friend, colleague, and roommate (now retired United Methodist Bishop) Woodie W. White reminded Ed King that "he had to think about what the

Christian church is and that the white southern Methodist church was not the only church in America." This, as Ed King describes, "opened my mind"[41] to a more inclusive understanding of the Church.

The motivation to plan was fueled by the desire for a new order of racial justice for all people. Ed King understood he had an obligation to Christ to pursue the desegregation of white churches in Mississippi, and one of the most important things for King was his gratitude that "Black people accepted me as a child of God with some potential."[42]

CHAPTER 4

Strategizing for Change

Most of the teachers who were at Millsaps during the time of the Interracial Fellowship left Mississippi and were banned from coming back. This was soon after Ed King (who was also told by the Mississippi Methodist Bishop at the time that he could not return) had graduated and enrolled in Boston University Theological Seminary.[43]

King and other students who had committed their lives to ending racial prejudice and injustice were now poised for action. It was time to strategize for change. At the outset of their planning, one thing was clear: this would be a strategy built on the foundation of non-violence with the intent of staging sit-ins at segregated restaurants, theaters, etc. in an attempt to stir the conscience of America to the injustices blacks faced daily.

Reconciliation is the main goal

In his autobiography, Ed King writes: "If these white Southerners–and their Black neighbor cousins–could ever overcome their past and their present, with Grace, the South might yet be the most favorable place for reconciliation to begin and spread through all America."[44]

Ed King found that reconciliation often failed when people could not get beyond their deeply rooted hate and discontent for one another. But racism and prejudice are still the two diseases that overwhelmingly hurt our world and hold us back from progress.

The white Christian churches in the South would prove most resistant to reconciliation. Earl D.C. Brewer, while speaking at the Southeastern Regional Consultation of the General Board of Education in 1964, said:

> Basically, the South is a region of traditionalism in transition. Some

> point with pride to the achievements
> of our forefathers. Others worship the
> "southern way of life" as a religion.
> Some view with alarm changes in the
> old patterns. Many are sovereign
> southerners before they are
> Americans–Americans before
> Christians.[45]

Already around the South, violence was
getting out of control as students who were
arrested because of protesting were beaten by
white police officers. Understandably, King
and other students feared that this could also
happen to them.

In addition, since America was segregated,
if white Christians in the South upheld such a
divide, then they were, by popular opinion,
being American in the best way.

In King's opinion, racial reconciliation in
Mississippi depended heavily on the
willingness of those perpetuating racial
injustice to "repent of their sins," reinforcing
his understanding that reconciliation was a
spiritual issue. In his autobiography, King
wrestles with the idea of reconciliation. He
says,

> And I wondered–can there ever be
> peace and reconciliation in Mississippi,
> in America, until the white man
> atones? Is the problem, then, that

white Mississippi must see its sins and confess its sins, and ask for forgiveness?[46] The strategy for change would include aspirations to bring about this kind of atonement and forgiveness–but things would get worse before they got better.[47]

What would work?

The immediate issue for King and his colleagues was "what strategies would work?" They maintained that the best route forward would be to prepare for and stage sit-ins in public venues. He and the students were given material on Ghandi to read that reinforced the importance of non-violence. King recalls the classes they took on sit-ins taught by Tougaloo professors and other civil rights leaders in Jackson. Obviously, their success would depend on how well they prepared.

Strategizing for change takes preparation with the focused attitude that something positive is going to emerge from the experience. The preparation, however, for King and his colleagues was just as painstaking as the actual sit-ins. They had to be fully prepared for the worst. King notes,

As we prepared for the sit-ins, I was given the role of the white policeman to play. Several black men and women were sitting at a mock counter with others acting in the roles of the waitresses. In role playing, I knew what my uncle, a Sheriff, and my cousin, a Deputy Sheriff, were like and so I went up to the counter and politely said, "you are at the wrong counter sir, and ma'am would you please go to your colored counter?" At this, Jim Lawson and all the others in the room collapsed with laughter because I was so loving and polite. They said to me, "During the sit-ins, the police may be violent."

The sit-ins started about 13 months later. King thought that it was wonderful that action was occurring and that they were in the heat of it. He wondered if the impact of the sit-ins would affect the white churches such that people would be non-violent and unafraid and that change would happen peacefully in Jackson.

This unfortunately did not happen. Chaos erupted in states like North Carolina, Louisiana, and Alabama as students joined the movement, were arrested, and were subsequently kicked out of their colleges.

In 1960, King took a leave of absence from seminary and went to Montgomery, Alabama, not long after to do behind-the-scenes work for the Movement for Reconciliation after reports that college students were being beaten by white police officers.[48] King recalls,

> There had been more violence (during the sit-ins and demonstrations) and police actually had machine guns out, but no press reported it. The women had been taunted and threatened and what I was to do was to try to get white clergy to get white laity to form a network to stop the police brutality and to get students reinstated into their academic institutions. This was the white class of people who might have been able to influence the city council and others."[49]

King began meeting with clergy from other denominations and gained an unexpected commitment from the Methodist Women in Montgomery who were willing to meet with black women if the Episcopalian and Presbyterian women came.

King also continued meeting with student groups (mostly white) touring the South. Though this was a dangerous commitment, King knew that the two groups who could also influence change in the South were white women and white students (non-southerners).

It was not long after organizing these gatherings that King was arrested. A police raid on the black-owned Regal Cafe at lunch on March 31 found King in company with a student group from MacMurray College in Jacksonville, Illinois, and local black activists, some of whom were affiliated with Martin Luther King Jr.'s, Southern Christian Leadership Conference (S.C.L.C.)

Twenty people in all were arrested and found guilty of disorderly conduct–behavior "calculated to create a breach of the peace," Judge D. Eugene Loe stated. Local press coverage of the story described the racial situation taking shape inside the cafe, led by white Illinoisans and Ed King ("a minister from Boston," according to the *Montgomery Advertiser*) with police officers arriving on the scene just in time to spoil the plans.[50]

Howard Thurman told Ed King one day after class at Boston that he should not expect anything like an ordinary vocation in the church.[51] After King's first arrest, he realized the accuracy of Dr. Thurman's words. King emerged from the arrest unbowed, telling reporters in Alabama that the arrest of the integrated diners came about because "police state conditions" prevailed under Governor John Patterson's rule.[52]

King discovered that demonstrations could take place on a smaller scale as well. Hours after his first arrest, he decided to invite a fellow clergy friend to have lunch at the Jefferson Davis Hotel where he had been residing during his time in Montgomery.[53]

He asked the hotel manager if he could bring a fellow clergyman to lunch and to the manager's surprise, the clergyman that King invited was his black friend Elroy Embry. The two were arrested as they attempted to dine in the Plantation room at the Jefferson Davis Hotel–King's second arrest.

King found that when arrested, a platform for commentary on racism and injustice was presented. After his second arrest, King commented to reporters from *The Today Show* that "the long days of chopping wood and cutting grass, supervised by guards riding horseback on the roadside, caused him no despair; on the contrary, he had been 'morally strengthened' by this attack on the 'idol of segregation'."[54] King realized that demonstrations worked, and when done correctly, could be the catalyst for major change.

Christians must be about change

Because of his arrests in Montgomery, King made the local Jackson, MS, newspapers' front page with his picture accompanying the headline, "Mississippi Methodist Minister on

Convict Road Gang."[55]

Convicted by work undone in Mississippi, King wrote to a ministerial colleague serving near his hometown. "There is still one other possibility. If I want to be a minister of the Christian Church and if I really believe the Christian Church offers the only possibilities of any real solution to any problems, then I must broaden my conception of the Christian Church–and even of the Methodist Church."[56]

The one thing that did not waiver was King's conviction that the Christian Church–with all of its flaws–would serve as the agent of change in a racially segregated society. His mission was clear, but even he would experience personal change along the way.

Not only must Christians who perpetuate racial division be willing to change, but the minister must also be willing to undergo a transformation in thought and at times, in process. Ed King would experience a change in process after returning back to Jackson to a situation of hostility towards his family.

Because of King's involvement with the sit-ins and other demonstrations that made national news, his parents were forced to leave their home in Vicksburg and ultimately the state of Mississippi. King, even after he returned to Mississippi, was under such scrutiny and in such danger that he and his wife moved for a short time to Montana until things calmed down.

He did not expect to take a hiatus from the movement, but he realized that he could not be as effective under the present conditions in Mississippi, and if he stayed, he had a high likelihood of being killed.

King recalls a life-changing experience of grace from a fellow black prisoner while working on the road gang after his first arrest. There was one water station and the white men on the road gang would go to drink first. King intentionally, but discretely, was the last white man to attempt to drink. When it was his turn, the officer refused to let him get a sip. King says,

> The white prisoners knew who I was and what I had done with regards to civil rights. The white men had their own cups to drink from while the black men on the road gang each shared the same tin cup. After I was refused a drink, I asked the officer, "After they are finished, can I have a drink of water?" to which he said, "no." The last black prisoner who had the tin cup graciously looked at me and said, "Here, Reverend King, take my water." The officer immediately tried to step in and tell him that I couldn't have his water and the black prisoner replied,

"I've had enough water, this man has done the same work that we have, he can have my share." And the officer did not beat him.[57]

King, at this point, understood that it was not just the college-educated individuals who were striving for change in a segregated society, but even those at the bottom of the social structure could in some way be agents of change. This came through showing grace and love towards others following the example of Christ.

If a black man on a road gang would risk his life to give King a cup of water, how much more could King give back to help others in the struggle for civil rights? This is the question that remained with him through the course of the ensuing demonstrations and struggle to bring about a spirit of reconciliation between blacks and whites.

CHAPTER 5

Demonstrating for Change

Ed King, other ministers, and civil rights leaders would be immersed into a struggle like nothing they had imagined. In December of 1958, teachers at Boston arranged for Ed and a few of his classmates to meet Dr. Martin Luther King Jr., a former student of Boston University. Ed, of course, could not tell anyone about these meetings, but they were instrumental in how he would come to understand his role in the Civil Rights Movement.[58]

Ed King, on occasion, would have lunch at

Dr. King's home in Montgomery and many of the questions he had regarding his vocation in civil rights were answer by Dr. King. Ed recalls hearing a sermon Dr. King preached in Montgomery titled, "Paul's Letter to American Christians" which brought he and other colleagues into a better understanding of what American Christians should be striving for in racial reconciliation.[59]

Several white men and women clergy who knew Ed King encouraged him not to come back to Mississippi because of the heightened racial tension. They admired his work in Alabama, but Mississippi was an entirely different landscape.

King would eventually return to Mississippi, and under special provisions from the Chair of the Board of Ministry, was able to be ordained an elder in the Methodist Church, but not given Conference membership. King became more active with his friend Medgar Evers, and in January 1963, he was appointed as Chaplain of Tougaloo College.

This would ultimately provide King an opportunity to organize black and white students to participate in demonstrations and to educate them on the importance of equality and reconciliation.

The strategy to change the segregated practices in Mississippi was clear—those committed to the movement would stage well-planned social demonstrations. King taught that racial reconciliation would not occur without action and faith. Those participating in the demonstrations also had to be extremely committed to the cause. With King and other civil rights workers in place, the demonstrations intensified in Jackson, Mississippi.

Woolworth's Sit-in

Ed had been working closely with students from Tougaloo and surrounding colleges to plan and stage a sit-in similar to the one in North Carolina at the Woolworth's lunch counter. Anne Moody was one of the young demonstrators who participated in this violent sit-in. She writes:

> I had become very friendly with my social science professor, John Salter, who was in charge of NAACP activities on campus. All during the year, while the NAACP conducted a boycott of downtown stores in Jackson, I had been one of Salter's most faithful canvassers and church speakers. During the last week of school, he told me that sit-in demonstrations were about to start in Jackson and that he wanted me to be the spokesman for a team that would

sit-in at Woolworth's lunch counter.[60]

Those who participated in the sit-ins had to be disciplined and willing to give their lives for the cause of racial justice. Anne Moody and others saw this movement as an opportunity that became a way of life. Strategy for these demonstrators was everything.

On May 28, 1963, to divert attention from the sit-in at Woolworth's, the picketing started at JC Penney fifteen minutes before. The pickets were allowed to walk up and down in front of the store three or four times before they were arrested.[61] Demonstrators were almost guaranteed to be arrested for any kind of participation, but this was the sacrifice they had to be willing to make.

At 11:15am, Anne Moody and two other demonstrators were occupying seats at the Woolworth's lunch counter. Anne says,

> In the beginning the waitresses seemed to ignore us, as if they really didn't know what was going on. Our waitress walked past us a couple of times before she noticed we had started to write our own orders down and realized we wanted service. She asked us what we wanted. We began to read to her from our order slips. She told us that we

71

> would be served at the back counter, which was for Negroes. "We would like to be served here," I said. The waitress started to repeat what she had said, then stopped in the middle of the sentence. She turned the lights out behind the counter, and she and the other waitresses almost ran to the back of the store, deserting all their white customers.[62]

Though they sat peacefully, their actions were radical. At the time, dining facilities were strictly segregated. A white mob arrived. Some Tougaloo students were beaten, and one was knocked unconscious. Others were doused with ketchup, mustard and sugar.[63]

During the sit-in, however, Moody and the demonstrators were given a glimpse of hope.

> There were five or six other people at the counter. A couple of them just got up and walked away. A [white] girl sitting next to me finished her banana split before leaving. A middle-aged white woman who had not yet been served rose from her seat and came over to us. "I'd like to stay here with you," she said, "but my husband is waiting."[64]

The news stations interviewed this woman. "When asked why she had said what she had said to us," Moody recalls, she replied, "I am in sympathy of the Negro Movement."[65]

Small glimpses of light such as this woman's confession were proof that the consciences of individuals were being convicted by the attention brought to the struggle for human and civil rights of blacks in America through the demonstrations.

Moody and other young demonstrators remained at the lunch counter and were met by the lunch crowd consisting of white students and local business people. The white male students taunted them and with the rope used to section off areas of the store, one tied a hangman's noose and attempted to put it around the demonstrator's necks.

The situation kept escalating, bringing in more angry white citizens to Woolworth's attempting to defend their segregated way of life. Sitting at the counter watching the chaos, the three Tougaloo students began to pray.

Moody says at that point, "All hell broke loose."[66] Memphis Norman, one of the lunch counter demonstrators, was thrown from his seat and subsequently kicked in the head by one of the white men in the mob. Memphis and his attacker were arrested.

As the situation intensified, others such as Joan Trumpaur, a white female activist, joined the lunch counter sit-in, was called a "white nigger" and lifted from the counter by the mob and taken out of the store. She found her way back into Woolworth's and the mob became angrier.

Moody writes: "Soon Joan and I were joined by John Salter, but the moment he sat down he was hit on the jaw with what appeared to be brass knuckles. Blood gushed from his face and someone threw salt into the open wound.

Ed King, then Tougaloo's chaplain, rushed to him."[67]

King was in the midst of the chaos that day and provided the transportation for the Tougaloo students from the Woolworth's store to safety at the NAACP headquarters on Lynch Street in Jackson. He also had a more strategic role during the Woolworth sit-in.

> The Rev. Ed King, a white Methodist minister who was Tougaloo chaplain in 1963, went to Woolworth's as an observer. During a 2009 AP interview, King recalled that he reported to Evers what was happening. "I had to call him and tell him that of the first sit-inners, a mob has formed, Memphis Norman was unconscious on the floor, he had been kicked ... had blood in his nose, I think even his ears. And he did have a

concussion from it," King said. "And the first two women had been dragged by the hair." Evers had to decide whether to keep the sit-in going and whether to ask others to join the two women who remained at the counter." Medgar has more courage than any of us," King said. "He knew he would be blamed."[68]

This was the kick-off to a series of demonstrations that would bring awareness to the unjust social condition of blacks in Mississippi. Certainly, the brutality took its toll on those who were demonstrating. Anne Moody expresses:

> After the sit-in, all I could think of was how sick Mississippi whites were. They believed so much in the segregated Southern way of life, they would kill to preserve it. I sat there in the NAACP office and thought of how many times they had killed when this way of life was threatened. I knew that the killing had just begun. "Many more will die before it is over with," I thought. Before the sit-in, I had always hated the whites in Mississippi. Now I knew it was impossible for me to hate sickness. The whites had a disease, an incurable

disease in its final stage. What were our chances against such a disease? I thought of the students, the young Negroes who had just begun to protest, as young interns. When these young interns got older, I thought, they would be the best doctors in the world for social problems.[69]

The momentum of the demonstrations carried over from privately owned companies to government entities. The night after the Woolworth's sit-in, a mass rally sponsored by the NAACP was held. Following the rally, a six-man delegation of black ministers was chosen to meet with Mayor Thompson to present him a number of demands on behalf of blacks in Jackson.

They were: hiring of Negro policemen and school crossing guards; removal of segregation signs from public facilities; improvement of job opportunities for Negroes on city payrolls–Negro drivers of city garbage trucks, etc; encouraging public eating establishments to serve both whites and Negroes; integration of public parks and libraries; the naming of a Negro to the City of Parks and Recreation Committee; integration of public schools; and forcing service stations to integrate restrooms.[70]

Prayers in Public

Ed King and other ministers decided to stage a "pray-in" at the post office in Jackson. King did not think they would get arrested because it was federal property.

> By the time we got to the post office, the newsmen had already been informed, and a group of them were standing in front of the building blocking the front entrance. By now the group of whites that usually constituted the mob had gotten smart. They no longer looked for us, or for the demonstration. They just followed the newsmen and photographers. They were much smarter than the cops, who hadn't caught on yet.[71]

King and others understood the message it would send if they were arrested for trying to pray peacefully in a public place–especially since they now had the full attention of local and national media. Even at this stage in the demonstrations, King and his colleagues intentionally kept a balance of white and black demonstrators. At the post office demonstration, there were fourteen activists present–seven whites and seven blacks.

Moody remembers the scene vividly.

We walked out front and stood and bowed our heads as the ministers began to pray. We were immediately interrupted by the appearance of Captain Ray. "We are asking you people to disperse. If you don't, you are under arrest," he said. But if we had dispersed, we would have been torn to bits by the mob. The whites standing out there had murder in their eyes. They were ready to do us in and all fourteen of us knew that. We had no other choice but to be arrested.[72]

Ed King and some of the other ministers who were kneeling refused to move; they just kept on praying.[73] After all of the demonstrators were arrested, news spread about the event and the energy and spirit of change spread to a local Jackson high school–Lanier High School. Four hundred students started singing freedom songs on their lunch hour and ignored the bell to return to class. They just kept singing.

The principal of the high school did not know what to do so he called the police and told them that the students were about to start a riot. All four hundred of the students were arrested, taken to the fair grounds and put in a large cell.

Anne Moody notes,

> When the cops came, they brought the
> dogs. The students refused to go back
> to their classrooms when asked, so the
> cops turned the dogs loose on them.
> The students fought them off for a
> while. In fact, I was told that mothers
> who lived near the school had joined
> the students in fighting off the dogs.
> They had begun to throw bricks, rocks,
> and bottles. The next day the papers
> stated that ten or more cops suffered
> cuts or minor wounds. The papers
> didn't say it, but a lot of students were
> hurt, too, from dog bites and lumps on
> the head from billy clubs.[74]

This "activist spirit" spread from Lanier
High School to Jim Hill, Brinkley, and other
local area schools, and students gathered on
Farish Street ready to go to jail. Ed King and
other leaders in the movement knew that their
strategy was working and that students and
citizens, both black and white, were energized
for change. Within five days, Jackson became
the hotbed of racial demonstrations in the
South. Those who did not go to jail were
considered cowards by those who did.[75]

Because of the magnitude of the
demonstrations occurring in less than a week

in Jackson, a local judge issued an injuction prohibiting demonstrations by the NAACP, CORE, Tougaloo College, and various leaders including Ed King. The next day, the injunction was answered with a mass march.

Mass rallies in Jackson became an every night event, and at each one the NAACP had begun to build up Medgar Evers. Medgar had become the face of the Civil Rights Movement in Mississippi similar to Martin Luther King Jr. in Alabama.

There was an indescribable momentum that had the segregationist system in Mississippi on its heels. However, on June 11, 1963, the Jackson movement would be dealt a great blow.

Medgar Evers was shot and killed in his driveway after returning home from an integration strategy meeting. His untimely death would test the resolve of the movement for racial equality and those who participated in it.

What would they do without their leader? Who would take the place of Medgar Evers? Evers had provided leadership to the Jackson movement with an unwavering commitment to reconciliation and justice that grew out of his experiences of brutality towards blacks in his early years.

When he was only 14, Evers observed to his horror the dragging of a black man, Willie

Tingle, behind a wagon through the streets of Decatur, Mississippi. Tingle was later shot and hanged.

A friend of Evers' father, Tingle was accused of insulting a white woman. Evers later recalled that Tingle's bloody clothes remained in the field for months near the tree where he was hanged. Each day on his way to school, Evers had to pass this tableau of violence. He never forgot the image.[76]

It was his tireless commitment to see this type of irresponsible killing cease for good. This commitment fed into his organizing efforts on behalf of the NAACP. He worked to promote the growth of adult-led chapters and to encourage involvement of younger activists in local youth councils across the state.

The inclusion of youth, Evers believed, was critical to a winning strategy in the crusade against Jim Crow. Under Evers' leadership, the NAACP doubled between 1956 and 1959 from about 8,000 to 15,000 dues-paying activists.[77]

Replacing a prophetic leader like Evers would seem impossible. But the Jackson Movement continued in the same spirit that Evers promoted–the spirit that hoped for a better day for blacks in the South and around the world.

CHAPTER 6

Freeing the Soul

The Civil Rights Movement teaches us that faith is authentic when it stays close to the ground. It reminds us of faith's essential affirmations: showing hospitality to strangers and outcasts; affirming the dignity of created life; reclaiming the ideals of love, honesty and truth; embracing the preferential option of nonviolence; and practicing justice and mercy.[78]

After the death of Medgar Evers, King knew that something needed to be done on a deeper level. They had made progress with demonstrations in social environments, but the real change would need to take place in the most guarded place in people's lives–the church. The underlying issue with many churches today, as it was in Mississippi in the 1960's, is that we have taken the Good News of God's love that is supposed to burn through racial and social divisions and turned it into a religion that reinforces the status quo.[79] The status quo King faced was the protection of a segregated way of worship that validated a segregated way in society.

The souls of Christians perpetuating segregation needed to change. One of the most lasting effects of racism on white churches is an intellectual wound that makes people think they will do right if they believe right, so they put all of their emphasis on believing the right things.[80]

In this case, however, the "right thing" was a misunderstood perception of the Kingdom of God and its *inclusive* nature of all people under the authority of Jesus Christ. Doing the right thing for white churches in Mississippi, before integration, meant protecting their way of worship and being and not having them corrupted by the inclusion of other races into their *sacred* space.

Dr. W.B. Selah, pastor of Galloway Memorial Methodist Church in Jackson, MS from 1945-1963, wrote an open letter to the Freedom Riders in 1961 addressing the issue of segregation in the church. He writes:

> It is not sinful for white people to prefer to worship with white people or for colored people to prefer to worship with colored people. The sin comes when a church seeks to put up a color bar before the Cross of Christ. As Christians we cannot say to anybody, "You cannot come into the house of God." To discriminate against a man because of the color of his skin is contrary to the will of God.[81]

Dr. Selah, even in 1961, had the understanding of Church correct; however, in practice, Galloway and other white churches in Jackson were far from living what the Bible teaches as the nature of the Church. Many black and white supporters of integration were still turned away from white churches and often arrested because of the perception that they were coming to cause a disturbance and interrupt worship.

Church Visits

Ed King's argument for an inclusive society did not lean on the concept that all races needed to be forced to worship together. However, if someone of a different race wanted to worship in any congregation, they should not be denied access because of their race.

This was the same principle he stood by with regards to public facilities and institutions. It was simply an issue of *access*; that any individual, regardless of race, should have access to places of worship and areas open to the public.

Because the demonstrations had drawn so much attention to the conditions in Mississippi and the South, King's strategy of integrating churches would need to unveil a racism that hindered blacks from worshipping Jesus in spaces where they were the minority. King wanted a proactive effort from all people to live together in a way that promoted the love of Jesus Christ and excluded division.

Civil Rights activist John Perkins suggests that it can be hard for white folks to see how race continues to hold them captive. This makes it hard for them to accept the freedom Jesus offers in God's Kingdom.[82]

Freedom is the key: freedom to worship, and freedom to live. King pushed for inward freedom. The soul of a person needed to be free from the sin of hatred towards another. If souls were free from hatred, America would be a better place for all its citizens.

Ed King, students, and other activists would attempt to promote the understanding that "even while we were his enemies, Christ died for us. That's the greatest love you'll ever know, and it has the power to transform both our lives and our society."[83] They would call all people to a commitment for a better and more just society.

Perkins believed that in history, every good movement calls people to commitment. Every good movement inspires each individual to make sacrifices for the greater good; and every good movement invites people into something greater than themselves– something they would not be foolish to sacrifice everything for.[84]

King and others would plan to visit churches in Jackson that they knew would not grant them access in an attempt to expose a racism that transcended exclusion from restaurants or theaters; this was the church–a place where all should be welcome.

Medgar Evers had the last conversation about his life with Ed King a couple of hours before he died.[85] While the Jackson movement was progressing, Medgar had taken a group of people to First Baptist Church and they were turned away.

This church was on television each Sunday, and notoriously racist Governor Ross Barnett taught Sunday school there. Several of the women with Evers began crying on the steps of the church because they realized that the hatred was so deep, that they could not attend church with people of a different race.[86] The sentiment was, "There is no hope if white people won't even let us pray together."[87]

Medgar then took the same group of people to Galloway and the television cameras from First Baptist followed. For the second time on the same Sunday just minutes apart, the nation had seen a group of people, black and white, turned away from a church because of their race and stance on equality.[88]

That same day, trying to handle the situation at the front door, Dr. Selah collapsed from a bleeding ulcer in the church hallway. Medgar was killed two days after visiting Galloway church.

In response to Medgar's death, Blacks in Mississippi non-violently said, "You can put us in prison and we'll keep coming. You can kill our leaders and we'll keep coming. You can beat us and shed our blood and we'll keep coming."[89]

Students at Tougaloo College primarily would rally together and the lead the charge for what Ed King deemed as the "Church Visit Campaign." After the conflict at Ole Miss over integration and the admittance of its first black student, James Meredith, in 1963, the violence of the Klan intensified to try to stop efforts of the civil rights activists to integrate other arenas–especially churches.

Charles Marsh, on the Church Visit Campaign, writes:

> Ed King and company went straight for the jugular. Sunday after Sunday, he and his theological comrades appeared on the steps of Jackson's most segregated white churches, praying, singing, testifying—enacting time and again spectacular scenarios that teased out of the "church guards" darkly comic and ironic assertions about faith and social existence. As the campaign proceeded during the fall of 1963 and spring of 1964, it had all the makings of a theater of the absurd wherein the myriad theological contradictions of a closed and racist society became evidenced and pantomimed.[90]

As the Klan intensified its terror, civil rights activists pumped up the pressure for change in Mississippi. In 1963, as King began challenging segregation at whites-only churches in Jackson, he would bring groups of Tougaloo students to the steps of white churches and ask to be let in. The black students were almost always refused.[91]

King says, "The idea was to appeal nonviolently to the best of the white community."

"Underneath it all were the theories of the American dilemma, that if you can show the contrast between the reality and the American dream then you have a resource in all the American people for change."[92]

Ed King believed that the church visits would spark a reasonable, interracial dialogue that would lead to greater progress and reconciliation. King recalls,

> On the steps of churches, many denominations, blacks and whites would talk for fifteen or twenty minutes. The doors [of the church] would be closed and then people would say, "What would Jesus do? What's your religious teaching for this?' For six or eight weeks there were whites who would tell the ushers, "I don't think I can worship here today," and go home.[93]

The Jackson Citizens' Council moved to crush the church-visit campaign. In October 1963, Jackson police began arresting blacks and whites involved in the "pray-ins" at the churches. King and his students continued their radical crusade.

On one autumn morning, they came to Galloway Church on Communion Sunday. The "church guards" were not ready this Sunday and Ed King and students began banging profusely on the church doors to the point that it interrupted those taking communion at the altar.

Marsh notes,

> Triumphant, King's vexing reply was aimed to agitate. "If we can't worship the same God together inside the same church buildings, then we will still knock on your door and so irritate you that you cannot worship your white God in peace, that you cannot escape thinking about the problems of segregation even on Sunday morning; for we are letting you know that every single aspect of your Southern way of life is under attack.[94]

King himself was a large part of the campaign's fascination: a tall and wiry man of indefatigable energy, he made himself a menace to every white minister who presided over a segregated parish.[95]

Theologically, the presence of blacks on the outside of white congregations being refused entry made congregations wrestle with the authenticity of their claims on the gospel and their Southern way of life. What the church visits were accomplishing at this stage was an intense awareness of how

"Godly" [white] people misrepresented the teachings of Jesus by perpetuating segregation in worship.

This weighed heavily on many of the congregants in these churches as well as the pastors that led them.

If people could begin to realize their sin, they could change. King, then, knew that their work was successful. The underlying concept was that souls become free when they are convicted to change.

If the soul of a person was held hostage by racism and prejudice, then the conviction that the Holy Spirit brings was the answer to the soul gaining freedom from such oppressive emotions.

In the epilogue of his book, *The Preacher King: Martin Luther King, Jr. and the Word that Moved America*, Dr. Richard Lischer suggests, "In America, [Martin Luther King] announced that oppressed people can seize the rights that are due them without losing their soul in the process or destroying those who abuse them.[96]"

Ed King and those participating in the church visits would have to find the balance between conviction and destruction. They wanted to destroy the evil of segregation and injustice, not the people fostering such evil.

As the Freedom Summer movement gained more traction, a menacing event occurred that would again test the resolve of the activists. On June 16, 1964, the White Knights of the KKK killed three civil rights workers in Philadelphia, Mississippi: James Chaney, Andrew Goodman, and Michael Schwerner. After that, Ed King says he lost faith in trying to appeal to the white community.[97]

Ed King delivered the eulogy at the memorial service for James Chaney, and he condemned white moderates for not just tolerating, but helping to foster flagrant racial injustice. "These people are just as guilty as the 'sick white Mississippians' who carried out the brutal murder, and more damned in their souls because they know it's wrong,'" King said.[98]

Speaking at the memorial service for James Chaney gave Ed King a national stage from which he could express the cause of their push for racial reconciliation. Many people had died for their belief in a more just and inclusive society, and the brutal murder of the three civil rights workers in Philadelphia further expressed this point.

When would white Americans realize that the way of segregated life was not only wrong, but also deadly? Even in asking this question, King discovered that often in the struggle for racial equality and reconciliation, lives would be lost in pursuit of a greater purpose.

Forgiving Moral Failure

Looking back, King blames Mississippi whites for moral failure. He includes those who fought to preserve segregation and those who remained passive.[99] Speaking on the timidity of white churches, King says, "They had to worry about losing their resources. It became self-defense very quickly."

King remembers a rabbi whose home was bombed in Jackson because so many Jewish students were involved in the Civil Rights Movement. He says such events had a chilling effect on the rest of the white community.[100]

Eventually, King had to come to forgive the moral failure of whites who helped preserve a segregated society, committed injustices against blacks, and also those who were passive. He would begin to understand that forgiving the moral failure of others is an essential component of racial reconciliation.

For Lischer, the church exists at the center of the dramas of the civil-rights movement: not the church as described in so much conventional wisdom as an instrument of social change ("a supportive social environment," in Charles Payne's words), though it undoubtedly is that, but rather the church as the body of Christ, the "colony of heaven" (in Martin Luther King's words) where the costly demands of the prophets and Jesus are preached without compromise.[101]

Ed King desired the church to present a clear and authentic picture of the body of Christ and pay the cost of breaking down barriers of division in a racist environment. Individuals with the most influence in society would, however, need to leverage their stimulus to a cause more meaningful than segregation. In King's view, their energy was being wasted on preserving a way of life that displeased God and brought shame to the body of Christ. In the words of Charles Marsh:

> The convictions and commitments that animated the movement will need to be rescued from ambiguity and equivocation. Dr. King's final eschatological intensities—"Now the judgment of God is upon us, and we must learn to live together as brothers or we are all going to perish together as fools"—confront us with a severe and chastened hope.[102]

Learning to live together would require the ingredient of forgiveness. Certainly, segregation and the unjust society that King and others lived in would not be forgotten as history continues to remind us of the struggle daily.

However, in light of history, progress can

be made towards reconciling the past in hopes of a more glorious future as brothers and sisters in Christ when the soul is free from the sins of racism and prejudice.

CHAPTER 7

Eschatology and Racial Reconciliation in American Christianity

Christians in America should seek racial reconciliation as our main goal to ensure a holy transition into more diverse congregations as ethnic demographics in our country change. On the subject of *Embracing God's Passion for Ethnic Diversity*, Randy Woodley writes:

> We need a plethora of perspectives and cultural worldviews if we are to see a

clearer picture of the immense grandeur of our Creator God. The truth is, once we get close enough to any people group–or, for that matter, any person–we usually discover that many of our initial observations were based on false assumptions. Primarily we assume that everyone else in the world is "just like us."[103]

Among the many reasons *why*, Woodley suggests that we often look at people negatively who are different than us because we have not been taught to appreciate the diversity of other people and cultures.

The narrative of American history is filled with the devaluing of people from different ethnicities. Deeply rooted in our country is a disdain for those who are *different* and those who do not fully represent our often skewed depiction of the American dream.

American Christian life has also taken on this quality and in the process, has made the Church exclusive of racial and ethnic diversity on a large scale rather than inclusive. That is not to say that there are not many American church communities accepting diversity–for these we give thanks. But for the majority of American Church communities in the 21st century, diversity has not been accepted or promoted. This is not to presume that

American churches are not willing to accept diversity, however, most have not taken the step in this direction.

According to research from Dr. Michael Emerson (co-author of *Divided by Faith: Evangelical Religion and the Problem of Race in America*) recorded in The Christian Post article, *Race Relations, Affirmative Action, and the Church* by Ed Stetzer, 92 1/2 percent of churches in the U.S. are racially segregated (with 80 percent or more of the congregation comprised of a single race or ethnic group).

Dr. Emerson also notes that churches are 10 times more segregated than the neighborhoods they are in, and 20 times more segregated than nearby public schools.

If we use these statistics as a measure for racial inclusivity in American Christian Life in light of the coming wave of diversification in America, then many American church communities are in trouble.

The reality is, American communities as early as 2020 will begin seeing significant changes in ethnic structure. Consequently, as communities change, so must churches.

Moving beyond a history of racism

What the Church Visit Campaign in 1963-64 tried to convey was that Christians are much stronger together than we are divided. It also began the conversation on how we as Christians in America must move beyond our past of racism and hate in hopes of gaining life together looking towards eternity.

Racial reconciliation encompasses an acceptance of the past without allowing history to dictate the outcome of the mission that Jesus Christ calls Christians to through discipleship.

The Church in the 21st Century will have to embrace racial equality in a way it refused to during the 20th century and before. All people must be welcomed in all places of worship and for the sake of the gospel, be treated with dignity, respect, and as equals. Here, I want to suggest how this can be done.

First, American Christians should realize that racial diversity is a good thing and special gift from God. There are over seven hundred references to ethnic groups in Scripture. Seeing color is not ungodly, and the Bible does not ask us to give up our ethnicity or to replace it with some generic notion of non-ethnic Christianity. [104] Jesus himself embraced his own ethnicity. Alvin Sanders says:

> Ethnic borders are cultural traits that define our ethnic identity for ourselves and others. Today, Christians are one in Christ, but our ethnic differences do not pass away with salvation. Christ's

goal was not to eliminate ethnicity but to transcend it. Organizations that accept ethnicity as a normal part of the human experience will acknowledge, appreciate, and leverage differences instead of denigrating or ignoring them. These organizations would be following in the footsteps of our biblical forbearers.[105]

Ed King and those who planned and demonstrated for change did not demand that whites in Mississippi or the entire U.S. give up their ethnic identity or culture; they just wanted to be accepted as equals. America's struggle to move beyond a history of racism has become the Church's struggle as well. But this is nothing new.

Throughout the biblical record, we see a theme of struggle, discrimination, and conflict: one story after another of individuals and ethnic groups trying to advance their own interests over others.[106] Though we are different, the main interest Christians in America–regardless of race and ethnicity– should be advancing is the saving and reconciling message of Jesus Christ.

Moving beyond a history of racism also means that no one ethnic group can claim superiority over another. Equality becomes a priority and fellowship a great reward. When constructing a sense of identity, we must recognize that we are always partly unique and partly a creation of our society. These two aspects can never be isolated from each other.[107]

This was displayed excellently in the relationship between white and black civil rights activists. Whites involved in the Civil Rights Movement did not try to be black, or vice versa.

However, they tried (and in many ways succeeded) to live equally with one another and fight for the same cause, although they were each uniquely designed by the Creator and uniquely formed by their society. Even more, they did this with the understanding that whites in America operated in certain privileges that blacks did not.

Ed King became close friends with Medgar Evers in a racially tense and divisive environment. Moreover, Medgar Evers, given Ed King's childhood history in Mississippi, accepted him as a brother.

Their relationship and their subsequent actions taken to bring about change in America depict how two people of different ethnicities from different places can move beyond a divisive history towards a cause greater than themselves. The Church will have to do the same.

Shifting from a Homogeneous to Heterogeneous Perspective of American Christianity

A consequence of segregation that continues today is a perspective of the Christian Church in America that lives in homogeneity and often shuns diversity. Because of our history, distrust for people of different races still abides.

However, the shift from homogenous to heterogeneous American Christian communities will depend primarily on how and the rate at which racial reconciliation occurs.

One of the main issues, however, is that many do not feel passionate about pursuing reconciliation in hopes of a more diverse reality in Christianity. Or, some begin the conversation, and because of impatience with the long process of healing and confrontation with the past, abandon the cause all together.

Alvin Sanders says it this way: "The pattern goes something like this. An organizational desire arises to either start or advance the process of becoming multi-ethnic. Task forces and committees are formed and meetings happen, producing a vision of some sort. This vision of what could be is predominant and the major driving force."[108] How, then, does the shift occur?

Ed King's approach to keeping the most pressing issues in front of the people is key. The sit-ins and church visits were successful because those who were passionate about equality kept the bigotry and inequality in front of the people who needed to change the most.

Those who perpetuated racism were eventually worn down by their own hatred for blacks and those who were associated with the movement. Change came at the hand of spiritual and social conviction.

Such is the case with racial reconciliation today. The issues that foster racial division must remain in front of the people who most oppose diversity as well as those who start work towards reconciliation and quit.

To this, John Perkins suggests:

> Our churches have done little more than reproduce and radiate this brokenness of our culture. Where the church has grown in numbers over the past generation, it has been captivated by the "homogenous unit principle." This church-growth strategy says people are more likely to come to a church where most of the other people are like them. So pastors in the suburbs catered their services and programs to middle-class "seekers." And they built

big churches of middle-class people. Short-term mission trips became the main connection between these churches and poor people. Which means the poor aren't members of our big churches. They're out there somewhere, in need of help. A whole lot of our churches have decided to outsource justice. If the gospel of reconciliation is going to interrupt the brokenness in society, our churches are going to have to rethink their vocation.[109]

It is ultimately about how people are spiritually convicted in the sense of realizing the oneness of the ecclesia, and how they are socially convicted to withstand the hostility that may come with pursuing racial reconciliation. This, too, will also differ geographically.

Because most of the harsh crimes against blacks occurred in Southern states, it will perhaps be more difficult to make the shift in this region of the country, but not impossible. This also suggests that some groups will have to work much harder at racial reconciliation than others mainly because of history.

Many of us are tempted to say, "Racial inequities just happened. I am not responsible."[110] The contrary, however, is true. We are all responsible. Maybe not for the things done in the past, but for inequities in the present, we are responsible. An unwillingness to pursue racial reconciliation is a major inequity.

Christians in America will have to assume responsibility for our actions if the shift to more diverse congregations is going to occur as community demographics change. This coming shift will affect *how* racial reconciliation is pursued. To achieve this, I propose that certain elements must be present.

1. Relationships Strengthened through Prayer

Throughout the gospels, we are given glimpses into the prayer life of Jesus Christ. Though we are not sure in all instances *what* he prayed for, we do know that prayer was a vital part of his relationship with God. So influenced was Jesus about prayer, when asked by his disciples *how* they should pray, Jesus takes the time to teach them the way to communicate with God in order to strengthen their relationship with humanity. We know this as The Lord's Prayer.

A key verse in this prayer digs into the most intimate and intimidating aspect of life–

that is, forgiveness and reconciliation. Jesus instructs them to ask God to "forgive them their trespasses, as they forgive others who trespass against them (Matt. 6:12)."

It is interesting that the Savior places forgiveness of our sins and the sins of others in the most fundamental of prayers. Perhaps it is because in the context of prayer, a relationship with God is strengthened, but also relationships with other human beings are salvaged and rebuilt.

Ed King and those involved in the Civil Rights Movement understood prayer as a means to relationship building. Prayer gave them courage and strengthened them individually and in their relationships with one another. Having *pray-ins* was an intentional strategy that got at the heart of reconciliation in a segregated society.

If people could pray together, regardless of their differences, then maybe a more just society could be established and the walls of division would crumble. On the other hand, if people refused to pray together, like many did during the Church Visit Campaign, then that indicated that reconciliation was not a priority and that the walls of division would remain, at least for that time.

Such is the case for Christian communities in America today. If prayer becomes an avenue to relationship building, lasting relationships will be formed that will ultimately strengthen Christianity as well as the places where this transformation is occurring. As a result, accepting diversity will not be a struggle but a welcomed addition.

When we can do as Jesus taught and forgive those who have hurt us, then we can build authentic community regardless of race. Prayer essentially unveils racism in a way that brings the individual to personal repentance and then extends the grace of God towards another who has committed an injustice.

2. Realities Built on Trust

Proclaiming the gospel of Jesus Christ prompts us to invite people into authentic relationships where they can be restored to the beloved community and work for the common good of all. People, however, will not feel welcomed to such a restoration if they cannot trust those within the Christian community.

Without a doubt, the Church is the place where restoration takes place. It is a community of believers where the Holy Spirit is present. Prayer leads us into a reality necessary for racial reconciliation and trust for our fellow brothers and sisters.

Ed King modeled that one could begin to trust when one accepted the other for who they are.

Prayer and relationship building led to this level of trust.

Medgar Evers and Ed King were from two different ways of life and they accepted each other as equals. *Equality* has for many years been the issue. From Paul's arguments in Galatians about freedom and equality among the Jews and Gentiles, to the struggle for equality among blacks and whites in the 20th century to today, equality is and will be the backbone of trust.

This is why leaders of the movement fought so radically for equality. It is what Barbara Brown Taylor calls "radical trust." She says:

> This rock-bottom trust seems to come naturally to some people, while it takes disciplined practice for others. I am one of the latter, a damaged truster who hopes she has lots of time to work up to the advanced level before her own exodus comes. To that end, I keep my eyes open for opportunities to get slightly lost, so that I can gradually build the muscles necessary for radical trust.[111]

People since the first century have struggled with trust, and we should expect a struggle as well. Trust is built and actively pursued.

As Taylor suggests, some people trust easier and sooner than others; however, if racial reconciliation is a step to the greater goal of increased diversity in our churches, then the often painstaking work of learning to trust will need to be a priority.

3. Respect Driven by Love

One of our biggest problems as Christians is that we want the miracle without the love. We want to see the kind of healing Jesus brought, but we often miss Jesus' way of loving broken people.

Jesus performed signs and wonders here on earth, but he was also clear that the sign of the church ought to be love: "By this everyone will know that you are my disciples, if you love one another. (John 13:35)"
Love is supposed to be the abiding sign of the church.[112] Shifting a culture in a Christian community will not happen without love.

Christians are born to love–it is a part of our DNA. Ultimately, Jesus' call for us is to allow love to transcend all barriers of race and culture. Ed King loved those with whom he was in the struggle for civil rights, and they loved him.

The biggest challenge after they succeeded in getting churches to desegregate was loving the people who for decades kept them alienated from the house of worship–those who were mostly the perpetrators of injustice.

Heterogeneous churches will need *love* at their core. Love that is patient in learning different cultural norms, love that is accepting of things and people that are new. This is not to say that love is not a struggle at times, however, it is necessary.

For Dr. Martin Luther King Jr., what made him great was his determination that others should not be harmed in the struggle. When he said, "Freedom is not given, it is won," many people would have taken it as a cue to take up arms.

Dr. King taught instead that people should stand up for themselves, but with love and understanding for those who stood against them. He recognized that our enemies can be our greatest teachers.[113]

When Christian communities welcome diversity (especially for the first time), they should stay open to the possibility that some people might be hurt by comments, facial expressions, or even the unintentional outcasting that comes when individuals flock to whom they are most comfortable.

But learning to love is often uncomfortable. It makes us move beyond ourselves and embrace others. And a part of that love, as demonstrated in the Civil Rights

Movement, is for those who are new to the community to stand up for themselves in a way that doesn't create greater division, but in a way that magnifies love in spite of others' shortcomings.

The reason why prayer, trust, and love are key to racial reconciliation here on Earth is because there is a "world to come" in eternity with God where prayer, trust, and love will abound. Ed King and others understood this as a core teaching of the movement.

The life to come, as Ed King understood, would not be separated by race or culture–it will be the ultimate experience of Christian diversity. And for King, if heaven will be like this, then Christians on Earth should hold heterogeneous Christian communities as a proud mantle on display for the world to see.

CHAPTER 8

A New Vision for American Christian Life

The life of Reverend Edwin King provides a significant model for a heterogeneous vision for Christianity in America. Pastors, local churches, students, civic leaders, and citizens can apply this model in an attempt to broaden the conversation about racial inclusivity and the change in social demographics in the United States.

The way forward for the Church must include a more inclusive understanding of the Church universal in the sense that no one is denied access to any local church because of their race.

In a changing society, Christians, in order to keep the Church a thriving movement in the world, should apply Ed King's model of Spiritual and Social Conviction and Intentional Planning while promoting an Eschatological Perspective of diversity in Christian communities.

Applying Spiritual and Social Conviction

Ed King and other civil rights leaders understood if the consciences of people fostering segregation could be convicted, then change would occur. But it had to be a combination of both spiritual and social conviction. If a person was not convicted in their hearts to change, then chances are, they would continue to uphold the status quo.

Ed King, therefore, appealed to the Spirit within Christians as well as entities within society. Christians today must be willing to challenge the status quo and expose the spiritual and social wrongs associated with excluding people of different ethnicities from places of worship.

For example, Randy Woodley, on the topic of churches targeting certain demographics of people writes:

One pastor, following the plan as set forth in a nationally known bestseller in the area of church growth, told me that the group of people he was trying to reach was those with an annual income of more than one hundred thousand dollars. True to his intended purpose, his church is growing at an incredible rate and is full of wealthy white people. Although I credit the pastor and staff with genuine friendliness to all people, it is unfortunate that anyone from another race or with a lower income can spot these self-imposed standards on the very first visit to the church–which is also likely to be the last. And although we bask in the comfort of being around those very much like us, diversity is a gift from God.[114]

By law, segregation is illegal in the United States today, but many Churches are instituting (whether intentional or unintentional) practices that continue to promote segregated worship. Christians cannot be so obsessed with "church growth" that we compromise the gift of diversity that God offers and that his call requires us to pursue.

Churches like the one Woodley mentions

will continue to worship with people in a certain economic class and of a certain race until they are spiritually convicted to change and cast a wider net.

Spiritual conviction suggests that casting a wider net to include more people is actually a calling from God and a privilege for the Church. Pastors and Church leaders today must keep this as a core conviction– acknowledging that the Kingdom of God is larger than their plans to target certain demographics of people in order to "grow their church" using their own rules.

We do not build the Church on our plans, but on God's. And as communities change, so must plans for church growth. To this, Woodley suggests:

> Sometimes our theological approach to missions is indeed startling, particularly in the eyes of those who believe that non-Western, "uncivilized" peoples are unaware of God in their lives before a missionary comes on the scene. Those with a narrower focus seem to believe that God has His eyes fixed solely on Europe, and that the rest of the peoples of the world are outside His purview. According to the Bible, God did not wait to show up with the European

missionaries. In fact, Paul states in the first chapter of Romans that both righteousness and judgment have been revealed to all people, and that everyone has a chance to know God.[115]

This should be the core principle that leads to spiritual conviction. That is, "that everyone has a chance to know God" and the church is the place where anyone should be able to come and discover the God who created us all in God's image and who is able to transform us all.

What Ed King and others found was those perpetuating segregation in the church were also the same people perpetuating segregation in society. From restaurant owners to barbers and hairdressers, there was a societal division that would not allow for the acceptance of diversity and equality in the Church. In other words, how could people of different races worship together if they could not eat a meal, watch a movie, or socialize in the same place? Social structures had to change as well.

As communities diversify, so will the social arenas within those communities. Whereas people were used to only seeing a certain race in a restaurant, they will begin to see people from other races eating in those restaurants as communities change.

This is not limited to socioeconomics. Affluence in America today spans across the ethnic spectrum, and therefore Blacks, Whites, Hispanics, Asians, and others have the same opportunity to live where they want.

Perhaps it is even more difficult to admit that, when he so chooses, God can use those outside our established faith communities as much as He can use us. But God truly is at work in the world, not just in the Church.[116]

This is why Ed King believed that people should be socially as well as spiritually convicted. If their perspective of being with those different from them in society changed, then they would be more willing to accept such a change in the life of the Church.

In other words, if people who are different can attend the same movie theater or restaurant, then they should be able to attend the same church.

Applying Intentional Planning

If the success of the Civil Rights Movement proved anything, it proved that planning is critical. Ed King, students, and other civil rights leaders chose to make planning a priority in their efforts towards racial reconciliation and justice. Communities engaging in racial reconciliation cannot go into the process without a plan.

Several things to consider are:

- How will the planning affect social arenas in the area?
- Who will lead the conversations on reconciliation and the subsequent events?
- To what length is the congregation and community willing to go to be inclusive of people of all races?

There must be an end goal in mind. For instance, Ed King understood that if the church could desegregate and be an example, then segregated social structures would fall as well. So he and others planned their demonstrations around the ultimate goal of desegregating white congregations in the Mississippi.

Therefore, the sit-ins, pray-ins, street demonstrations, and countless meetings were steps towards the end goal of church desegregation.

Dr. Martin Luther King Jr. was conscious of his need to collaborate with sympathetic whites, especially those who identified themselves as people of faith and with whom he presumably shared a common commitment to the values of peace and reconciliation.[117] Christian communities, therefore, cannot neglect the importance of intentional planning if racial reconciliation is going to occur.

As progress in planning is made and results are produced, there will be the temptation to say, "We have done enough." To this, Edward Gilbreath writes:

> Back in the day, "Negroes" were simply expected to know their place in society as the inferior race and to accept it. Today the feeling among many white Americans is that people of color, and particularly African Americans, should be satisfied with the tremendous advances in race relations since the civil rights period, and that to bring up perceived inequalities is to expose oneself as either a whiner or a race baiter. Race, as both a social construct and a visible reality, is the gigantic elephant in the American living room that some insist will disappear if only we would just ignore it. For African Americans and other people of color, however, it is difficult to ignore a six-ton pachyderm when it's sitting on top of you.[118]

Ignoring racial division will not bring about racial reconciliation, especially since this cause is still important to most minorities in America. Christians should not settle for *enough* in relation to racial reconciliation and should not ignore the difficulty involved in building new relationships in spite of an adverse history.

In her book that seeks to uncover the hidden forces that keep Christians separate, Christena Cleveland writes:

> I chose to build community with people with whom I could pretty much agree on everything. I invested lots of time and energy in fostering relationships with people who had similar ethnic backgrounds, were about my age, possessed similar educational degrees, professed similar theology, worshiped like me, voted like me and were fluent in the language of my postmodern, intellectual, influential, wanderlustful, "diverse" culture. I sincerely thought that I was doing a fabulous job because, hey, I was "living in community," and isn't that what good Christians are supposed to do?[119]

It takes intentional planning to avoid having a compartmentalized perspective of Christian community like Cleveland suggests during periods of racial transition. This can be difficult because at some point, the task of racial reconciliation becomes tiring and often seems like progress is not happening.

During the Church Visit Campaign, when Ed King and others who wanted to accept diversity were turned away countless times, they got tired and often thought that progress was not happening. But intentional planning also suggests that congregations press through the painstaking elements of the plan with the understanding that the end goal will help build the body of the Christ.

Applying an Eschatological Perspective

This brings me to the most critical point of this model: applying a perspective of the Kingdom of God and the life to come to the task of racial reconciliation.

Everything that the Christian Church does hinges on our perspective of the Kingdom of God and the life that Christ will reward to us after we pass from this life to the next.

In his *Letter from a Birmingham Jail*, Martin Luther King, Jr. responds to criticism from religious leaders in the South about his leadership in the struggle for civil rights. Gilbreath suggests:

Their names are not familiar now, but the eight ministers were each influential and respected in their corners of Birmingham, and were among some of the most prominent religious leaders in the state of Alabama during that time.

They weren't just local pastors, but regional bishops and national officers of their denominations. So, for them to add their names to such a document made a statement.

Though they were all technically "moderates," the eight white clergy represented a sundry collection of social philosophies and religious expressions. Still, they found unity around the belief that demonstrations like King's would only lead to hostility, violence, and further civil unrest.[120]

What they did not realize, however, is that the movement was built on frustration towards the racist establishment's push to suppress the hostility, violence, and civil unrest that affected whites in the South through the demonstrations.

They failed to consider the hostility and violence that Blacks were continually subjected to daily. This was not just physical hostility, but also spiritual hostility.

Thus, Dr. King responds in an articulate and firm way explaining the plight of Blacks in the South (specifically in Birmingham) and his spiritual conviction to continue the fight for racial reconciliation and justice in view of the life to come. Perhaps one of the most notable expressions from Dr. King in his letter is when he writes:

> But more basically, I am in Birmingham because injustice is here. Just as the prophets of the eighth century B.C. left their villages and carried their "thus saith the Lord" far beyond the boundaries of their home towns, and just as the Apostle Paul left his village of Tarsus and carried the gospel of Jesus Christ to the far corners of the Greco Roman world, so am I compelled to carry the gospel of freedom beyond my own home town. Like Paul, I must constantly respond to the Macedonian call for aid.
>
> Moreover, I am cognizant of the interrelatedness of all communities and states. I cannot sit idly by in Atlanta and not be concerned about what happens in Birmingham. Injustice anywhere is a threat to justice everywhere. We are caught in an inescapable network of mutuality, tied in a single garment of destiny. Whatever affects one directly, affects all indirectly. Never again can we afford to live with the narrow, provincial "outside agitator" idea.

Anyone who lives inside the United States can never be considered an outsider anywhere within its bounds.[121]

If one Christian community chooses not to fully engage in racial reconciliation, it affects the entire body of Christ. Dr. King was clear that blacks and whites should be working towards the same goal. Certainly Ed King was convinced that Christians of all races had a place in the Kingdom of God.

Their message, like Jesus', was direct: we must work for a cause greater than ours individually. That is, that all people might receive the salvation that Jesus Christ offers and live together in authentic community in this life and the life to come.

Pastors and church leaders should teach and promote an eschatological perspective of racial reconciliation in order to keep their community motivated for the task. If those involved in the Civil Rights Movement only worked for what was available in this life, I suspect they would not have made much progress.

However, their theology of the life to come was represented in the spiritual songs that they sang as they marched and demonstrated. Eschatology was the foundation of the Civil Rights Movement, and it must be the foundation of racial reconciliation in a heterogeneous vision for American Christian life.

Ed King, a quiet spirit, who selflessly led during the Civil Rights Movement and beyond, will be remembered for his prophetic voice and stance for the cause of Christ and justice for all.

But most of all, he will be remembered for his undying commitment to seeing the body of Christ flourish on Earth as we look towards a life in eternity with our Creator. In Ed King's own words:

> There were times we in the movement would say, "Wow, how can we be here at this moment?" And then we would remember and be thankful that we were, and you've been at one of these moments. We also talked of beloved community, and we never thought we, or maybe our great grandchildren if we had them, would live to see that but we absolutely believed it, and we said, "Nevertheless, or Hallelujah, tonight, we will hold hands and love each other because we will live in the kingdom now and in the eschatological." And we also could say, "How could it be us, at this moment?" and have a sense of awe, and a sense of the absurdity of it all, and that God is somehow able to

use all of that, and there was a joy in there, and a lot of laughter, so I want to give you a story of the absurd, at the moment, at the place, and maybe some joy.[122]

As the color barrier is broken and reconciliation is achieved, it may be absurd to some and impossible to others, but we seek a blessed hope in Jesus Christ that through our toil, God may be pleased with our work and our commitment to the Kingdom.

NOTES

1. Steven G. Carley, *Race, Ethnicity, and the United States' Demographics* (Boston: SGC), Kindle location 49.

2. Erica Frankenberg and Chungmei Lee, *Race in American Public School: Rapidly Resegregating School Districts* (The Civil Rights Project Harvard University), 2.

3. Andrew B. Lewis, *The Shadows of Youth: The Remarkable Journey of the Civil Rights Generation* (New York: Farrar, Straus and Giroux), Kindle location 43.

4. Jeffrey Lamar Coleman, *Words of protest, words of freedom: Poetry of the American civil rights movement and era: An anthology* (Durham: Duke University Press), 122-123.

5. Taken from: A memo written in April 1964 from a meeting of the Southern Student Organizing Committee in Nashville, Tennessee.

6. Gregg L. Michel, *Struggle for a Better South: The Student Organizing Committee, 1964-1969* (Palgrave: Macmillan), 45.

7. Taken from: The minutes of the 1963 SNCC Executive Committee Meeting, December 27-31 in Atlanta, GA.

8. Ibid.

9. Jack Minnis, *A Chronology of Violence and Intimidation in Mississippi Since 1961* (Atlanta: SNCC), 5.

10. Ibid, 8.

11. Kenneth Leech, *Race: Changing Society and the Churches* (New York: Church), 32.

12. Kate Ellis and Stephen Smith, *State of Seige: Mississippi Whites and the Civil Rights Movement,* a documentary by American Radio Works posted January 2011.

13. Charles Marsh. *God's Long Summer: Stories of Faith and Civil Rights* (Princeton: Princeton), 116.

14. Charles Marsh. *God's Long Summer: Stories of Faith and Civil Rights* (Princeton: Princeton), 116.

15. King, Ed. 2013. Interview by author. Jackson, MS. February 12

16. King, Ed. 2013. Interview by author. Jackson, MS. February 12

17. Charles Marsh. *God's Long Summer: Stories of Faith and Civil Rights* (Princeton: Princeton

University), 119.

18. Ibid, 119.

19. Charles Marsh. *God's Long Summer: Stories of Faith and Civil Rights* (Princeton: Princeton University), 120.

20. King, Ed. 2013. Interview by author. Jackson, MS. February 12

21. King, Ed. 2013. Interview by author. Jackson, MS. February 12

22. Charles Marsh. *God's Long Summer: Stories of Faith and Civil Rights* (Princeton: Princeton University), 120.

23. Ed King, *Be Not Afraid* (speech, Millsaps College, 2005).

24. Ed King, *Be Not Afraid* (speech, Millsaps College, 2005).

25. King, Ed. 2013. Interview by author. Jackson, MS. February 12

26. Kate Ellis and Stephen Smith, *State of Seige: Mississippi Whites and the Civil Rights Movement,* a documentary by American Radio Works posted January 2011.

27. Charles Marsh. *God's Long Summer: Stories of Faith and Civil Rights* (Princeton: Princeton University), 122.

28. Charles Marsh. *God's Long Summer: Stories of Faith and Civil Rights* (Princeton: Princeton University), 122.

29. Westley F. Busbee, *Mississippi: A History* (Wheeling: Harlan Davidson), 272.

30. Ibid, 278.

31. Ed King, *Be Not Afraid* (speech, Millsaps College, 2005).

32. Lewis, Andrew B. *The Shadows of Youth: The Remarkable Journey of the Civil Rights Generation* (New York: Farrar, Straus and Giroux), Kindle location 1410.

33. Ed King, *Be Not Afraid* (speech, Millsaps College, 2005).

34. Ed King, *Be Not Afraid* (speech, Millsaps College, 2005).

35. Ibid.

36. Medgar Evers, in John R. Salter, Jr., *Jackson, Mississippi: An American chronicle of Struggle and Schism,* Jackson, Mississippi: An American

Chronicle of Struggle and Schism," (Malabar, FL, 1987), 120-121. Also indicated as a part of King's speech at Millsaps College in 2005.

37. Clayborne Carson and Kris Shepard, *A Call to Conscience: The Landmark Speeches of Dr. Martin Luther King Jr.* (New York: Hatchette), 70.

38. Ed King, *Be Not Afraid* (speech, Millsaps College, 2005).

39. Ed King, *Be Not Afraid* (speech, Millsaps College, 2005).

40. King, Ed. 2013. Interview by author. Jackson, MS. February 12

41. Ibid.

42. Ibid.

[43] King, Ed. 2013. Interview by author. Jackson, MS. February 12

[44] Ed King Manuscript. Small Manuscripts (b1978.3) Archives and Special Collections, J.D. Williams Library, The University of Mississippi

[45] W.J. Cunningham/Galloway Church Papers. Small Manuscripts (b1978.6) Archives and Special Collections, J.D. Williams Library, The

University of Mississippi

[46] Ed King Manuscript. Small Manuscripts (b1978.3) Archives and Special Collections, J.D. Williams Library, The University of Mississippi, 128.

[47] Ibid, 128.

[48] King, Ed. 2013. Interview by author. Jackson, MS. February 1

[49] Ibid.

[50] Charles, Marsh. *God's Long Summer: Stories of Faith and Civil Rights* (Princeton: Princeton), 123.

[51] Ibid, 123.

[52] Ibid, 123.

[53] Ibid, 123.

[54] Charles, Marsh. *God's Long Summer: Stories of Faith and Civil Rights* (Princeton: Princeton), 124.

[55] King, Ed. 2013. Interview by author. Jackson, MS. February 12

[56] Charles, Marsh. *God's Long Summer: Stories*

of Faith and Civil Rights (Princeton: Princeton), 124.

[57] King, Ed. 2013. Interview by author. Jackson, MS. February 12

[58] King, Ed. 2013. Interview by author. Jackson, MS. February 12

[59] Ibid.

[60] Anne Moody, Coming of Age in Mississsippi (New York, Bantam Dell, 1968), 286.

[61] Anne Moody, Coming of Age in Mississsippi (New York, Bantam Dell, 1968), 286.

[62] Ibid, 287.

[63] Emily Wagster Pettus, *Miss. honors 50th anniversary of its Woolworth's sit-in,* The Associated Press, June 12, 2013.

[64] Anne Moody, Coming of Age in Mississsippi (New York, Bantam Dell, 1968), 287.

[65] Anne Moody, Coming of Age in Mississsippi (New York, Bantam Dell, 1968), 287.

[66] Ibid, 288.

[67] Ibid, 289.

[68] Emily Wagster Pettus, *Miss. honors 50th anniversary of its Woolworth's sit-in,* The Associated Press, June 12, 2013.

[69] Anne Moody, Coming of Age in Mississsippi (New York, Bantam Dell, 1968), 289.

[70] Ibid, 292.

[71] Ibid, 295.

[72] Anne Moody, Coming of Age in Mississsippi (New York, Bantam Dell, 1968), 295.

[73] Ibid, 296.

[74] Anne Moody, Coming of Age in Mississsippi (New York, Bantam Dell, 1968), 297.

[75] Ibid, 299.

[76] Dernoral Davis, *Medgar Evers and the Origin of the Civil Rights Movement in Mississippi*, Mississippi History Now, October 2003. http://mshistorynow.mdah.state.ms.us/articles/53/medgar-evers-and-the-origin-of-the-civil-rights-movement-in-mississippi

[77] Ibid.

[78] John M. Perkins and Charles Marsh, *Welcoming Justice: God's Movement Toward*

Beloved Community (Madison: InterVarsity), 20.

[79] Ibid. 36.

[80] Ibid, 40.

[81] W.J. Cunningham/Galloway Church Papers. Small Manuscripts (b1978.6) Archives and Special Collections, J.D. Williams Library, The University of Mississippi.

[82] John M. Perkins and Charles Marsh, *Welcoming Justice: God's Movement Toward Beloved Community* (Madison: InterVarsity), 40.

[83] Ibid, 44.

[84] John M. Perkins and Charles Marsh, *Welcoming Justice: God's Movement Toward Beloved Community* (Madison: InterVarsity), 48.

[85] King, Ed. 2013. Interview by author. Jackson, MS. February 12

[86] Ibid.

[87] Ibid.

[88] Ibid.

[89] King, Ed. 1980. Interview by John Jones. Jackson, MS. November 20

[90] Charles Marsh, *Jesus in Mississippi*, Books and Culture: A Christian Review, March/April 1998.

[91] Kate Ellis and Stephen Smith, *State of Seige: Defiance and Compliance,* a documentary by American Radio Works posted January 2011.

[92] Kate Ellis and Stephen Smith, *State of Seige: Defiance and Compliance,* a documentary by American Radio Works posted January 2011.

[93] Ibid.

[94] Charles Marsh, *Jesus in Mississippi*, Books and Culture: A Christian Review, March/April 1998.

[95] Charles Marsh, *Jesus in Mississippi*, Books and Culture: A Christian Review, March/April 1998.

[96] Richard, Lischer, *The Preacher King: Martin Luther King, Jr. and the Word that Moved America* (New York: Oxford), Kindle Locations 5084-5085.

[97] Kate Ellis and Stephen Smith, *State of Seige: Defiance and Compliance,* a documentary by American Radio Works posted January 2011.

[98] Ibid.

[99] Kate Ellis and Stephen Smith, *State of Seige: Defiance and Compliance,* a documentary by

American Radio Works posted January 2011.

[100] Kate Ellis and Stephen Smith, *State of Seige: Defiance and Compliance,* a documentary by American Radio Works posted January 2011.

[101] Charles Marsh, *Jesus in Mississippi*, Books and Culture: A Christian Review, March/April 1998.

[102] Charles Marsh, *The Beloved Community: How Faith Shapes Social Justice from the Civil Rights Movement to Today* (New York: Basic), 150.

[103] Randy Woodley, *Living in Color: Embracing God's Passion for Ethnic Diversity* (Downers Grove: Intervarsity), Kindle Locations 113-114.

[104] Alvin Sanders, *Bridging the Diversity Gap: Leading Toward God's Multi-ethnic Kingdom* (Indianapolis: Wesleyan), Kindle Location, 307.

[105] Ibid, 307-308.

[106] Ibid, 322.

[107] Alvin Sanders, *Bridging the Diversity Gap: Leading Toward God's Multi-ethnic Kingdom* (Indianapolis: Wesleyan), Kindle Location, 401.

[108] Alvin Sanders, *Bridging the Diversity Gap: Leading Toward God's Multi-ethnic Kingdom*